# FREIGHTM

## REVIEW

A DECADE
OF CHANGE
1995 TO 2004

**Martin Buck**

# CONTENTS

First published : April 2005

ISBN : 0-9537540-4-9

Published by : Freightmaster Publishing
158 Overbrook
SWINDON
SN3 6AY

01793 - 644957

Printed By : Stephens & George
MERTHYR TYDFIL

Cover design : Martin Buck & Artworking, PURTON

# ABOUT THIS BOOK

## Chapters

FREIGHTMASTER REVIEW is divided into periods of time which equate to the publication of each edition of FREIGHTMASTER; the front covers acting as chapter pages.

## Reference

This book is a 'diary' of freight with events chronicled in calendar month sequence, the majority of which have been recorded in FREIGHTMASTER. If you wish to cross-refer between the two publications, please note the relevant details will be found in the edition of FREIGHTMASTER published following the reference in this book.

On a technical note....

## Headcode

In most cases, the reporting headcode for each service is quoted, which is a reference used by Network Rail to keep track of trains. The full 'train i.d.' used by the TOPS computer consists of four characters and a full explanation of what makes up a headcode is given at the back of this book.

The letters (L) and (E) are used to identify whether a particular freight service runs 'Loaded' or 'Empty'. Also, some freight services start out running as a special ("Z") working before being allocated a 'proper' (Timetabled) headcode and, wherever possible, the 'proper' headcode is always given.

## Freightliner cum Intermodal

Freightliner and intermodal trains feature regularly in this Review, which are basically one of the same thing - a train conveying containers to/from British ports. Over the years, we have become accustomed to calling such services 'freightliner' (probably due to the fact Freightliner Ltd run the vast majority of container trains) but, as other operators have entered the container market, a distinction has been made to identify the respective services, thus:

Freightliner : Freightliner Ltd          Intermodal : DRS / EWS / GBRf

## Disclaimer

Every care has been taken to ensure accuracy during research and compilation although there may well be slight discrepancies in the chronology. If so, I apologise, but any such discrepancies should not detract from the general scheme of things.

Some readers may feel there are freight services / areas of the country included at the expense of others, which is also not intentional. Whilst this Review is not designed to be a comprehensive record of freight developments, it is intended to provide a 'snapshot' of some of the key developments which have help shape the railfreight scene during the currency of FREIGHTMASTER REVIEW.

# INTRODUCTION

*10 years and counting .....*

.....as, believe it or not, FREIGHTMASTER has reached a significant landmark in its history; it is 10 years and more than 35 editions since the first book appeared and we thought it would be a good idea to celebrate the occasion.

The result is this special 10th. Anniversary publication; a historical account of notable freight developments (and a few setbacks!) that have helped shape the rail-freight scene in this country during the last decade. I have also included some examples of 'short lived' freight trials that never quite came to fruition along with some 'one-off' workings, which ran for specific events, so as to give as complete a picture as possible of the decade in question.

The freight services documented in this narrative are all recorded in FREIGHTMASTER, the majority of which are backed up by high quality colour photographs, submitted by some of the most respected photographers in the country. My thanks go to all who have kindly contributed photographs for inclusion in FREIGHTMASTER REVIEW.

Whilst compiling this title, I was mindful of a phrase often bandied around by rail enthusiasts about the UK freight scene.... "Nothing ever changes". Well, I quickly discovered that in reality the scenario was completely different. Gone is the monolithic British Rail, replaced by new freight operators complete with their own locomotives and countless new air-braked wagons, which work new freight flows for a variety of customers on what is for the most part, a professionally-run and business-like railway.

*Background :*

To add a touch of perspective, it is worth taking a few moments and have a look at the development of FREIGHTMASTER itself.

FREIGHTMASTER is the brainchild of Mark Rawlinson, a Lancastrian, who has always been interested in railways along with a tangible association with timetables. However, it was whilst out and about videoing freight trains that Mark realised how useful it would be if there was a publication which listed passing freight services at a selection of locations around the UK.

Initially, the first timetable he produced was a list of freight services for the north-west stretch of the West Coast Main Line, which is perhaps not surprising when you consider that Mark lives close to the main line near Carnforth! Encouraged by both family and friends, Mark then set out to seek other freight timings from a variety of sources and compile some more timetables.

Having cobbled together a small selection of timetables, there then followed a frantic period of proof-reading and photocopying in readiness for publication.

An advertisement was placed in a railway periodical and the first few editions of FREIGHTMASTER went on sale during Winter 1994/1995 - a fledgling cottage industry had been launched, albeit with an uncertain future.

I first had the good fortune to catch sight of one of the early editions of FREIGHTMASTER in Summer 1995 during a visit to Milford Junction, which just happened to be the first time I had taken an active interest in railways for more than five years - a case of being in the right place at the right time!

I marvelled at the book's concept and potential.

Having met up with Mark in August 1995, we quickly decided that by bringing together our respective strengths, FREIGHTMASTER could be turned into a viable commercial concern. In practice, this collaboration means Mark concentrating his efforts full-time in developing the content of FREIGHTMASTER, whilst I look after the business from a managing and marketing perspective.

Since then, the book has evolved into a professional, quality product, which has seen 37 timetables increase in number to over 80 with three times as many pages, inclusive of an informative section detailing Freight Flows. FREIGHTMASTER is now published quarterly and has become the acknowledged 'bible' of freight with a widespread readership; not only railway enthusiasts, but professional people, such as engineers, noise consultants, town planners, etc, not to mention the freight operators themselves!

### Development :

A logical development took place in July 1997, when a sister companion (CLASS ONE) was published to bring together details of loco-hauled passenger trains in the UK; the book version being superseded by a computer based product five years later.

Whilst staying on the computer front, "FM Online" was launched in 2002 to complement FREIGHTMASTER; a new service enabling subscribers to 'download' freight timetables direct to a personal computer. FM Online has many benefits, including extra timetables and details of weekend engineering possessions / diversions, notwithstanding the fact that every timetable is regularly updated - some even on a weekly basis!

In addition, under the FREIGHTMASTER PUBLISHING umbrella, other projects have been implemented, such as our very own, highly successful, series of illustrated guides on the main railway lines in the country. So far, four titles have been published featuring the West Coast, East Coast and Great Western Main Lines, plus the old 'Midland Route'.

As to the future, we hope to make FREIGHTMASTER REVIEW a regular publication, but published more frequently, probably on a bi-annual basis - so watch out for future announcements!

Now, after 10 years of hard work and more than 80,000 copies sold, FREIGHTMASTER has become a household name in the rail-freight industry and a specialised railway publishing house in its own right.

So, without further ado, let's turn the page and have a look back at the decade's freight highlights and hope the next 10 years are as equally rewarding.

MARTIN BUCK

Freightmaster Publishing

April 2005

# SETTING THE SCENE

As we entered the 1990's, it is probably fair to say that railfreight was in the doldrums with freight haemorrhaging to road transport, wagonload services disappearing following the end of *'Speedlink'* and an uncertain future due to the Government's desire for railway privatisation.

With all this, one could argue that the future looked rather bleak but, out of adversity, a revitalised railfreight sector emerged, albeit slimmer and run by private companies. During this review we shall see how it all shapes up and to start us off, here is a 'snap shot' of the significant developments.

## Freight Operators

Operationally, the big change takes place in 1996 with the sale of British Rail's freight business to American firm Wisconsin Central with the deep-sea container business (Freightliner) sold to a management buy out. The new companies are known as English, Welsh & Scottish Railway (EWS) and Freightliner, respectively.

EWS eventually lose the responsibility of transporting nuclear waste in the UK to a new company, Direct Rail Services (DRS) who, in turn, extend their sphere of operations by working with W. H. Malcolm introducing new Anglo-Scottish intermodal services.

Another new freight operator enters the scene in 2001, Great Britain Rail Freight (GBRf), with their own distinctive 'Bluebird' livery class 66/7 locomotives, whose initial work is restricted to infrastructure trains but they later spread their wings and haul deep-sea container trains on behalf of the Medite Shipping Company.

## Operations

During the period, we witness the decimation of the British coalfield and the growth in imported coal and the movement of long distance coal flows from Scotland to English power stations. While EWS run the majority of coal services, Freightliner launch their 'Heavy Haul' division complete with their own class 66 locomotives and wagons and in just two years secure over 25% of the coal sector.

In fact, during the Review, Freightliner see the biggest increase in railfreight business, most of it gained at the expense of EWS, with the Company moving into new sectors, including automotive, cement, infrastructure and petroleum.

Another significant event concerns European freight with the opening of the Channel Tunnel in 1994 and a new freight marshalling complex at Dollands Moor, Kent, to act as the main centre for European operations; consequently, we see the end of the Dover - Dunkerque train ferry. EWS operate freight services through the 'chunnel' and as hazardous materials are barred, the main flows to/from Europe are automotive, 'Enterprise' and intermodal.

A major player in the railfreight market throughout the period is Royal Mail who, in conjunction with EWS, introduce new locomotives and rolling stock to haul mail trains across the rail network. Royal Mail also embark on a major capital programme to build eight new mail terminals strategically sited on the network and so remove mail handling at the majority of main line stations.

Unfortunately, this was all to end in tears as the Royal Mail and EWS sever their working relationship in 2004 and with it the end of 166 years worth of the Travelling Post Office and mail trains. The last night of operation features unprecedented public presence and interest, either to post letters for the special TPO handstamp or to quite simply witness the end of another era of rail history. However, there is a silver lining as GBRf start running mail trains for the Royal Mail using 325-units in December 2004, albeit on a trial basis until the end of the March 2005 - let's hope the trial is a lasting success!

Another development sees major retailers increasingly use rail to transport their goods around the country. Examples include Safeway (since taken over by Morrisons) who use the intermodal service to service their stores in the far north of Scotland, along with Asda, Argos and B. & Q. There is also Securicor who, in conjunction with EWS, launch a dedicated parcel service linking the Midlands and Aberdeen / Inverness.

## Infrastructure

From an infrastructure perspective, a major change takes place in 1999 when 'Local Distribution Centres' (LDC) are established around the country, where the formation of engineers trains will be handled, all of which having facilities for stockpiling ballast and spoil. This change sees the abolition of ad-hoc 'target' workings and the establishment of timetabled civil engineers trains.

Also, the period sees a welcome return of freight traffic to terminals accessed on previously closed/mothballed branch lines. Some notable examples include the reopening of seven miles of track on the Portishead branch serving Portbury Docks, plus the lines serving Birch Coppice and Chatham Docks.

## Rolling Stock

EWS introduce 'American-style' class 66 locomotives, leased from General Motors. With a fleet of 250, (christened the 'Red Death' by rail enthusiasts!) this spells the end for several locomotive classes in the EWS pool, including 31, 47, 56 and 58 - all surplus to requirements, even those in good operating condition!

The other freight operators soon follow suit and order their own fleets of class 66 locomotives, thus resulting in a universal 'standard' freight diesel locomotive, something which should have taken place following the end of steam 40 years ago.

As well as new locomotives, a plethora of new rolling stock comes on stream and following the withdrawal of vacuum braked PHV hoppers on the Tunstead - Northwich limestone circuit in January 1998, all freight trains (except some engineers trains) are formed of air-braked wagons.

Of unique interest is the launch of the 'Piggyback' wagon which enables an actual lorry container (wheels and all) to be carried by rail. Following a short-lived trial in 1997 for Milk Marque to convey milk containers from Penrith to Cricklewood, successful operations are established on behalf of Parcelforce

## In Conclusion

The UK railfreight sector has witnessed great change during the period 1995 - 2004, leading to a more competitive, profitable and efficiently run railfreight sector. We hope this will continue in the next ten years and we look forward to this with eager anticipation.

# THE 'RUN UP'

Before we turn our attention to the review itself, it is worth taking a brief look at a few key events prior to the publication of FREIGHTMASTER, which have a bearing on the ten years under review. In essence, the events relate to: (1) the impact on continental freight traffic in connection with the opening of the Channel Tunnel, (2) the reorganisation of British Rail's freight business leading up to privatisation and (3) Coal, the effect coal privatisation has in relation to rail.

## CHANNEL TUNNEL

### 1987 - 1994

The Channel Tunnel was one of Europe's biggest infrastructure projects. Work started in 1987, taking seven years to complete, at an astonishing cost of £9,000,000,000. The Tunnel has three tubes (2 rail / 1 service), dug by 13,000 engineers and workers, is 31 miles long (24 miles under the sea) at an average depth of 150 feet under the seabed.

*Right* : This picture helps to illustrate the scale of the project. At Grain TML depot, 33021 *Eastleigh* + 33051 *Shakespeare Cliff* depart from the terminal with the 1,000th. train of Tunnel segments in November 1990. (BM)

In connection with the Channel Tunnel, a new freight yard is built at Dollands Moor, Kent, which will be the UK base of Railfreight Distribution's (RfD) Channel Tunnel freight operations and the gateway to Europe. Wembley will be the European Freight Operations Centre and all services from UK terminals will run to Wembley. Similarly, there is a marshalling yard at Calais Frethun to handle European freight operations on the other side of the Channel.

In association with this, a new Eurocentral International Freight Terminal opens at Mossend, Lanarkshire, to be Scotland's rail freight link with Europe, operated by RfD. A class 47, No. 47245 was named *The Institute of Export* to mark the occasion.

## JUNE 1994

On 1st. June, the first freight service passes through the Channel Tunnel; a trainload of Rover cars for Milan, hauled by a pair of SNCF class 222 locomotives. SNCF will provide motive power to mainland France until new purpose built Class 92 locomotives come on stream.

*Right* : The two SNCF locomotives (22379 + 22403) wait at Dollands Moor with the first rail freight service through the Channel Tunnel. Class 47 No. 47323 *Rover Group* is also in attendance. (BM)

Initially, RfD will use a fleet of class 47 locomotives to work domestic trains between Wembley and Dollands Moor, usually in pairs, until the new class 92 locomotives become available for use in January 1996. RfD start running Intermodal services through the Tunnel: 3 services initially to France, Italy and a joint train to Belgium/Germany. This type of service conveys containers and 'curtainsiders' which can be transferred directly between lorry and train.

*Top* : A typical working in the early days of intermodal freight between Wembley and Dollands Moor .... a pair of class 47's (47229 + 47287) approach Kensington Olympia station with 4O64, Wembley - Dollands Moor, which is made up of both containers and 'curtainsiders'. (NG)

*Below* : The European Freight Operations Centre at Wembley Yard, seen at night in the class 92 era, where containers from continental destinations are remarshalled into domestic trains for Lawley Street, Mossend, Trafford Park, Wakefield and Willesden. In this view , 92023 *Ravel* waits to depart with a mixed consist bound for Dollands Moor ( to Melzo). (PS)

## ORGANISATION

### April 1994

British Rail restructure their freight business as part of the Government's privatisation plans by splitting Trainload freight in to three companies, based around a geographic division of current traffic. The companies are:

- North Freight
- West Freight
- South East Freight

Each Company has their own maintenance & servicing depots with a fleet of locomotives and wagons.

Changes also affect Railfreight Distribution (RfD), which comprises trains not aligned with the existing Trainload Freight sub-sectors of Coal, Construction, Metals and Petroleum. These will be absorbed by the new freight divisions leaving RfD to concentrate on Automotive, European and Freightliner operations.

### October 1994

Further reorganisation sees the three regional freight companies become three new companies with their own respective corporate livery:

- Loadhaul
- Transrail
- Mainline

Transrail launch '**Enterprise**': a network aimed at the long distance HGV market. Essentially, existing services from Cornwall and Kent to the north will be extended to link with those from the North East and South Wales and from Fort William and Inverness in Scotland, to provide an overnight network of long distance trains.

Warrington becomes the central 'hub' of the 'Enterprise' network, where portions will be exchanged between trains on the trunk Anglo-Scottish route. Bescot, Mossend and Wembley will be important 'staging' points for the trains and 'Feeder' services will also bring traffic to/from these centres from railheads and terminals around the country.

**Loadhaul** :  (ex - North Freight)

Black & orange livery with Loadhaul branding, probably the most striking of the new liveries.

*Above* : 56083 at Sudforth Lane, Kellingley.  (MB)

**Transrail** :  (ex - West Freight)

Two tone grey livery with Transrail branding.

*Above* : 31105 *Bescot TMD...* at Crewe Basford Hall. (CB)

**Mainline** : (ex - South East freight)

Two tone grey livery with a Mainline logo of rolling wheel imagery and bold black lettering.  Also, a bright blue livery with silver colour scheme.

*Above* : 58050 *Toton Traction Depot*  at Worksop West. (CB)

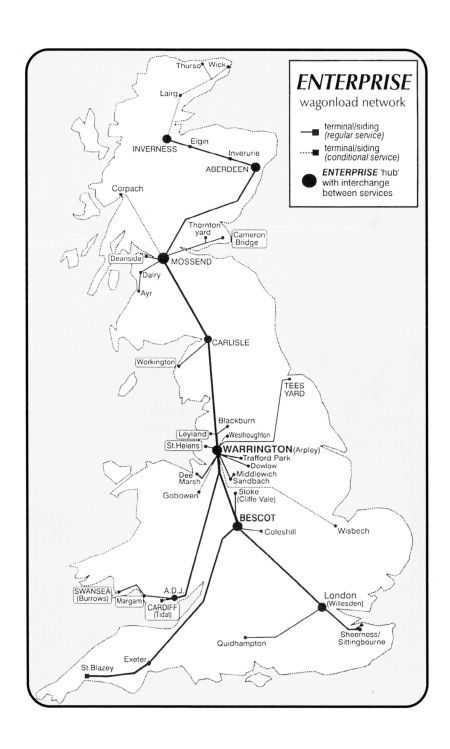

11

## COAL

### March 1994

A new railhead opens at Cwmgwrach washery in the Vale of Neath to receive coal from three private mines in the vicinity. Coal will then be transported to Aberthaw power station on a daily service using a rake of MGR HAA hoppers.

Class 37 No. 37703 hauls the first train on the branch and results in the first mineral line to reopen following post-Miners' strike closure.

### April 1994

National Power enter the freight sector. They introduce their own distinctive blue-liveried General Motors Class 59/2 locomotives (59201 - 59206) and a fleet of JHA bogie hopper wagons.

The locomotives initially start work conveying limestone from Tunstead to the desulphurisation plant at Drax followed by work on the Gascoigne Wood merry-go-round circuit, supplying coal to both Drax and Eggborough power stations.

A maintenance depot opens at Ferrybridge to service the locomotives and JHA wagons.

### October 1994

British Coal no longer exists, as almost all the English deep mining and opencast sites have been acquired by RJ Budge (Mining). One of British Coal's last acts was to close Silverwood Colliery, Rotherham.

Some good news! Transrail secure a contract to move imported coal from Grangemouth to Fiddlers Ferry power station. With more closures in the English and Welsh coalfield, this marks the start of a significant increase in the flow of Scottish and imported coal to English power stations.

*Above* : At Cwmgwrach, 37802+37898 *Cwmbargoed DP* await the completion of loading in order to leave with a supply of coal, 6C32, the 12:25 service bound for Aberthaw power station. (AK)

*Above* : The new rolling stock is a most welcome addition to the freight scene. After a run-round in the sidings, 59201 passes Milford Junction with a rake of JHAs forming 6D92, Tunstead - Drax. (JR)

*Above* : In between Greenhill Lower and Cumbernauld, 60066 *John Logie Baird* (still sporting Coal sector decals) passes Allandale at the head of 7M70, Grangemouth - Fiddlers Ferry. (IL)

# *FREIGHTMASTER*

### The complete guide to rail freight today

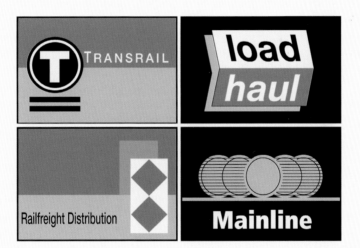

## January 1995 to February 1996

**FEBRUARY : Coal**

**(1) :** Loadhaul secure a contract to transport coal from Killoch Colliery via the Glasgow & South Western line to Blyth power station. The coal is 'tripped' to Falkland Junction Yard, Ayr, and the trains are worked to Carlisle by a pair of class 37s before handing over to a class 56 for the trip to Tyne Yard, thence to the power station:

    7Z84, Killoch - Blyth (L)                          6Z85, Blyth - Killoch (E)

**(2) :** Another new flow sees Loadhaul conveying household coal in Cawood's containers to Mossend and Aberdeen. The coal originates from the Yorkshire coalfield and is tripped to Tyne Yard where it goes forward to Millerhill in the consist of 6S71, Thrislington to Inverurie, lime train. Any empty containers return with the lime empties on the 6E67 service to Tyne Yard.

**Freight Terminals**

Two new terminals open for business this month:

**(1) :** Associated British Ports at Hull Docks open their new Kingston bulk handling terminal to handle the import of coal and other bulk products. The first service to use the terminal was hauled by 56039 (aptly named *Port of Hull*) on a consignment of coke bound for Foxton cement works.

**(2) :** Dallam freight terminal, Warrington, opens for business after it closed to rail some five years ago. John G Russell (Transport) Ltd, in association with Transrail, have leased the former BR Full Loads depot at Dallam from Railtrack. The intention is to develop the yard into a road/rail interchange terminal serving the North West with freight traffic being 'tripped' to/from Arpley yard linking into Transrail's Enterprise network.

**Construction Materials**

The freight-only branch to Tytherington, near Bristol, re-opens to traffic after being mothballed two years ago and Mainline secure the contract to move stone from ARC's Tytherington Quarry to Acton, Brentford and West Drayton.

**Locomotives**

The new Class 92 electric locomotives finally receive their safety certificate to allow them to begin work on Channel Tunnel freight trains. Initially, the locomotives work between Dollands Moor and Calais Frethun, with services from Dollands Moor to Wembley being hauled by pairs of class 47 locomotives.

**Petrochemicals**

The final trainload of bitumen was delivered by rail to the Lanfina depot, Preston Docks, with future deliveries being made by road instead. The empty tank wagons left the depot behind 37708 forming 7E84, Preston to Lindsey. Interestingly, the flow will recommence 10 years later, albeit on an irregular basis.

**MARCH**

**'Connectrail'**

Railfreight Distribution (RfD) launch its new European Contract Services business - 'Connectrail' - which ostensibly exists to feed traffic to the Channel Tunnel and Dover train ferry; gradually transferring business from the Dover - Dunkerque train ferry to the Channel Tunnel, which finally ceases operating in December 1995.

Like Transrail's Enterprise service, 'Connectrail' is a national wagonload network (see map *overleaf*) with Wembley being the 'hub' of the network with services 'connecting' at:

| Birmingham | : Washwood Heath | Crewe | : Basford Hall |
|---|---|---|---|
| Newport | : Alexandra Dock Junction | Scotland | : Mossend |

*Above* : Class 37 No. 37415 prepares to leave Tyne Yard with loaded Cawood's containers forming 6S71, Thrislington - Inverurie. The coal is actually bound for Mossend on this occasion having been tripped to Tyne Yard from Rossington earlier in the day. (PS)

*Below* : An example of a 'Connectrail service is illustrated here with 90130 *Fret Connection* heading south at Harrison's Sidings, near Shap on the WCML, with 6M79, Mossend - Bescot. (PJR)

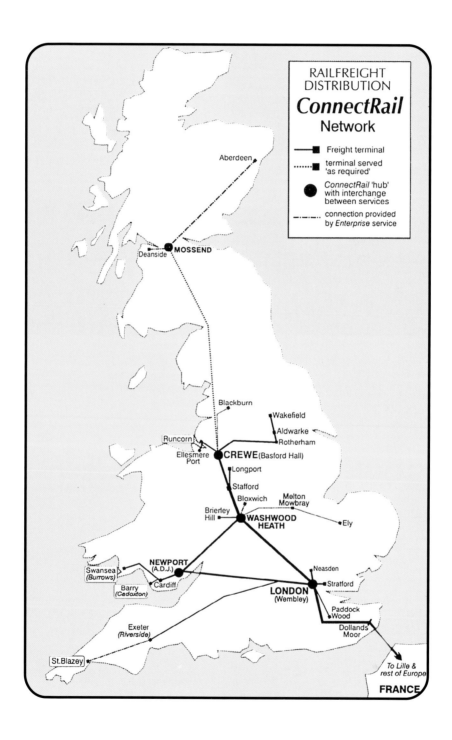

### MAY

### Coal

This month the movement of coal makes the news with four developments:

**(1)** : The last train from Kiveton Colliery runs this month to the colliery's only customer, Cottam Power Station.

**(2)** : However, on a more positive note, Annesley/Bentinck Colliery, under the control of Coal Investments Plc, has come back on stream having been mothballed for almost 18 months.

The first trainload of coal was despatched on the last day of the month to National Power's West Burton Power Station; ironically, all Bentinck's previous output had been taken by Powergen's Ratcliffe Power Station.

*Above* : At Annesley / Bentinck colliery, 58002 *Daw Mill Colliery* draws a rake of HAA hoppers under the loading bunker on the first day of operation under privatisation. (CB)

**(3)** : Triple-headers return to South Wales. Once a common sight on Port Talbot - Llanwern iron ore workings, triple headed class 37s make a brief return working MGR coal trains between Cwmbargoed and Aberthaw Power Station due to their superior braking capabilities over the previous class 56 operation.

The triple-headers were only required when using HAA wagons; pairs could work trains formed of HDA wagons due to their greater brake force and, in the end, the triple-headers were only required for the flow to Westbury cement works.

**(4)** : New Mainline blue-liveried MEA box wagons introduced, initially seeing use conveying coal slurry between Daw Mill Colliery and Rufford, replacing bottom discharge HEAs. These wagons will allow traffic to go places without bottom discharge (MGR) type facilities.

Also of note is that the very first MEA's, converted using HEA frames (and a couple of MAB's - converted using HAA frames) were painted in black and used on workings in South Wales, between Trelewis and Newport Docks.

## MAY (cont.) : **Automotive**

New double-deck car carriers introduced. These wagons are easily distinguishable due to their blue livery and unique design; each car carrier wagon being formed of five elements over 66 metres in length. A typical train set comprises of about 4 wagons.

*Above* : Passing Millmeece, just north of Norton Bridge, 90134 heads a rake of the new blue-liveried car carriers forming 6L42, Mossend - Dagenham. (RN)

## AUGUST : **Coal**

Transrail secure a contract with British Fuels for the supply of containerised coal to Inverness from Gascoigne Wood. This working sets out during daylight hours and provides a welcome source of new traffic over the Settle & Carlisle - the train is hauled by either a class 37 or class 56 and is made up of British Fuel's own distinctive red-liveried containers.

*Above* : The distinctive BNFL red containers help to identify 6M90, the (SO) Gascoigne Wood - Carlisle, as it passes Selside on the 'S. & C' behind 37087+37095. (RN)

**AUGUST** (cont.)

### Nuclear Waste

The final nuclear flask left Trawsfynydd nuclear power station bound for Sellafield and the end of traffic on the 'freight only' line between Blaenau Ffestiniog and Trawsfynydd. The final train, conveying two flasks, was hauled by a pair of class 31 locomotives, 31255+ 31199 suitably adorned with a headboard to mark the occasion!

### SEPTEMBER

### Coal

**(1) :** Mainline get a new coal contract following the opening by the Banks Group of a new opencast mine and railhead at Doe Hill, near Alfreton, which has a life expectancy of 5 years.

**(2) :** Not to be outdone, Loadhaul secure two new contracts. The first is the transportation of Sinter (a mixture of coke and iron ore pieces) from Teesside to Scunthorpe each weekday using HEA wagons:

   6D68, Redcar - Scunthorpe (L)         6N79, Scunthorpe - Tees Yard (E)

**(3) :** The second Loadhaul contract is the longest flow of coal on the rail network which involves the movement of coal from Killoch to the Castle cement works at Ketton.

The coal is moved in MEA box wagons and utilises one of the redundant paths of the Killoch to Blyth MGR services along the Tyne Valley. On reaching Tyne Yard, the train travels down the ECML as far as Peterborough.

*Right* : A pair of class '37s' are 'booked' to work this service and 6Z18, Killoch - Ketton, is seen passing Ruthwell on the ex-Glasgow & South Western main line headed by 37684 *Peak National Park* + 37884 *Gartcosh*. (PJR)

### 'Enterprise'

Freight services return to the Far North Line for the first time since the early 1980s. Transrail operate a new 'Enterprise' service, conveying steel for Georgemas Junction and containerised coal bound for British Fuels at Wick and Thurso:

  6Z55, Inverness - Georgemas Jct.
  6Z56, Georgemas - Inverness

*Right* : After arriving at Georgemas, any coal containers are 'tripped' to Wick and Thurso. Transrail-liveried 37430 pauses at Georgemas Junction awaiting the passage of 156474 from Thurso to Wick before leaving with the containers. (PJR)

## OCTOBER : Metals

**(1) :** After a gap of 5 years, freight traffic returns to the Metal Box factory at Westhoughton; any traffic being 'tripped' on an 'Enterprise' service, as required, from Warrington.

**(2) :** Additionally, also after a long break, freight traffic returns to Goole Docks with steel being 'tripped' to/from Doncaster, Sheffield or Rotherham for import/export.

*Above* : This panoramic view shows the docks complex at Goole with the quayside cranes dominating the background and 09014 marshalling the 6DO7 'trip' from Rotherham steel terminal, bogie bolster wagons laden with steel. (CB)

## NOVEMBER

### Freightliner

Thirty years ago this month, the first freightliner train ran from York way, London, to Gushetfaulds, Glasgow, and was (perhaps, surprisingly) the brainchild of Dr. Beeching. To mark this occasion, 47301 was named *Freightliner Birmingham* at Lawley Street, Birmingham.

*Right* : The named class 47 locomotive is seen hard at work passing Eaglescliffe hauling 4D87, Wilton - Doncaster Railport, freightliner. (PJR)

## DECEMBER : Petroleum

The 3-mile long Heathfield branch from Newton Abbott loses its last freight service following Gulf's decision to switch delivery to road; it was considered the 300 mile trip to be uneconomic. The last working was 6B21 petroleum empties to Robeston.

**DECEMBER** (cont.)

### Dover Train Ferry

A slice of unique railway operations pass into history as the Dover - Dunkerque train ferry ceases and means that all cross channel rail freight traffic must now use the Channel Tunnel via Dollands Moor.

On a historical note, the Southern Railway company and new SNCF invested in new train ferry docks at Dover and Dunkerque in 1931. The ships had rails on the cargo deck to carry railway wagons and carriages. Also, the luxury "Night Ferry" train had through coaches between London and Paris on this route.

*Right* : Albeit a black & white view , but I could not let this event go by without a pictorial record. The very last wagons are shunted aboard the MV *Nord Pas de Calais* Trainferry, propelled into the hold by class 08, No. 08831. (BM)

### JANUARY 1996

### Coal

National Power take over from Loadhaul the running of coal trains to its power stations at Drax and Eggborough using their own class 59/2 locomotives and bogie hopper wagons.

*Above* : In this panoramic view of the Gascoigne Wood complex, National Power's 59203 heads a rake of bogie hoppers alongside 56034 *Castell Ogwr/Ogmore Castle* on a traditional rake of MGR wagons. (JR)

# FREIGHTMASTER

## Spring 1996 Edition

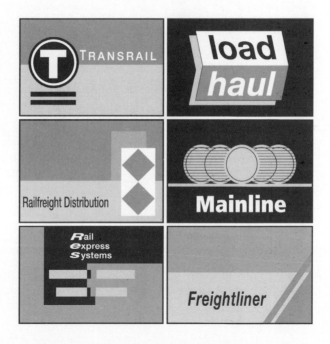

The complete guide to rail freight operations today

## MARCH : New Freight Operator

1996 will be an important year for railfreight operations with the first steps towards the Government's goal of a privatised railway network, starting with ....

### English, Welsh & Scottish Railway

British Rails' trainload freight operations - Loadhaul, Mainline and TransRail - sold to US based Wisconsin Central which, along with Rail Express Systems, will be united under the new operating name of English, Welsh & Scottish Railway (EWS). The first locomotive to carry the new EWS livery is class 37 No. 37057 *Viking*.

*Above* : The EWS house colours are maroon and gold and will be carried by the Company's fleet of locomotives and wagons along with place boards at EWS depots and yards, such as the one shown at the EWS yard in Workington. The EWS insignia is 3 animal heads: an English lion, Welsh dragon and Scottish stag, designed in conjunction with a competition organised by a leading railway periodical. (DMc)

*Top Right* : The first EWS liveried locomotive, 37057 *Viking*, enters Par station with 3 'twin' Cargowaggons forming a 'trip' service from Heathfield to St. Blazey. (AK)

## Coal

This month marks the end of the line for the Gwendraeth Valley coal line with March 29 seeing the last train (8B08, 11:00 Cwmmawr - Coedbach Washery) conveying anthracite coal which had been stockpiled at Cwmmawr Opencast Disposal Point.

This line was unique in that trains were worked by two class 08 shunters, which were fitted with headlights and had cut down cab roofs to work under the low bridges which have restricted clearances on the Burry Port & Gwendraeth Valley line.

Unfortunately, there are other casualties in the South Wales coal industry: Coedbach, Deep Navigation, Gwaun-Cae-Gurwen, Taff Merthyr, Trelewis, plus the last deep mine in Gwent at Oakdale.

*Right* : This is Cwmmawr Disposal Point and a view of 'cut down' 08994 *Gwendraeth*. The loading of HEA wagons was a fascinating process, whereby the loco. propels the empty wagons into the headshunt from where they are 'walked' down to underneath the bunker by a combination of humans and gravity.

Since this photograph was taken, the site has been completely demolished and the area is so full of weeds it's difficult to identify. (AK)

## APRIL

### Automotive

Following the 1995 prototype, the first batch of new KSA 'Cube' Wagons are introduced on the Swindon - Longbridge car body panel trains. This longstanding flow had previously used BR air-braked VAB, VBA and VGA wagons, followed by the current IZA twin Cargowaggons.

*Above* : The new 'Cube' wagons are shown to good effect in the consist of 4M08, Swindon - Longbridge car panel train, seen upon arrival at Washwood Heath, the automotive 'hub' of the West Midlands, hauled by 47286 *Port of Liverpool* + 47375 *Tinsley Traction Depot.* These trains being 'booked' a pair of RfD class 47 locomotives. The wagons, as they first appeared in 'ex-works' condition, are also illustrated on page 33. (PS)

### New Freight Operator - Direct Rail Services

The second new company to announce their intention to enter the railfreight market is Direct Rail Services (DRS), a British Nuclear Fuels Limited Group Company (BNFL) based in North west England. Their role will be to provide a safe, secure and reliable rail service in support of the movement of low level waste, bulk chemicals and irradiated nuclear fuel.

Operations will start in September 1996 using their own locomotives and, in the meantime, EWS will continue to work existing services until DRS come on stream.

### MAY : Freightliner

The third change of ownership is Freightliner; sold to a Management Buy-Out with the new company named Freightliner. Of note, is that some 70 locos and 345 freightliner flats were sold to Porterbrook Leasing and then hired back to Freightliner, enabling the new company to raise finance to purchase a further 40 locomotives.

Freightliner will run all internal container trains in the UK, plus a couple of other workings (aluminium ingots and Anchor butter) with the majority of services running to/from the ports of Felixstowe, Liverpool (Seaforth), London (Tilbury), Southampton and Thamesport (Grain). Most services convey 2 or 3 portions, which will be exchanged between services at Freightliner's main yard, Crewe Basford Hall.  Please see pages 25 and 159 for further details of these operations.

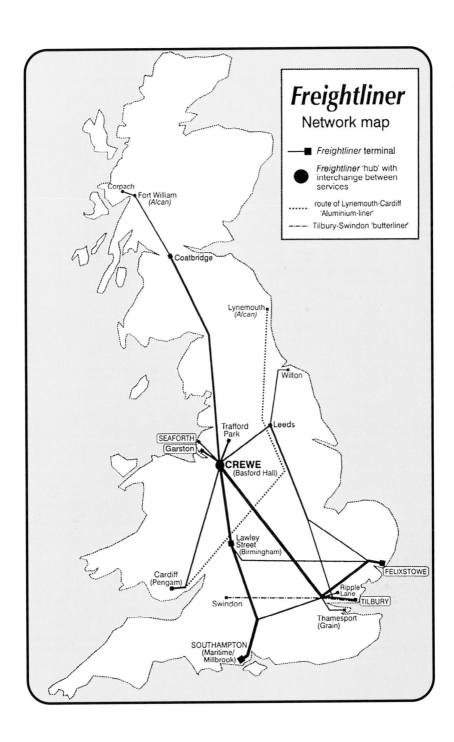

# FREIGHTMASTER
## Summer/Autumn 1996

The complete guide to rail freight operations today

## JULY : Locomotives

Permission is granted for the new class 92s to start hauling freight trains in the UK during the daytime between Wembley and Dollands Moor, albeit initially restricted to two return diagrams.

*Above* : The first member of the class, 92001 *Victor Hugo*, is pictured near Smeeth en-route to Dollands Moor with a rake of Cargowaggons, forming 6O56, Wembley - Dollands Moor (to Lille). (PJR)

## Automotive

Following the commissioning of a new car terminal at Corby, a flow of GEFCO car trains starts running from Dollands Moor, bringing in Citroen, Peugeot and Renault cars from France via the Channel Tunnel using cartics hauled by 2 x class 47 locomotives. The service is:

6M14, Dollands Moor - Corby (L)          6O49, Corby - Dollands Moor (E)

*Above* : With a burst of acceleration, 47335 + 47362 pollute the air as they make their way through Bedford hauling 6M14, the Dollands Moor - Corby imported cars. (NG)

**JULY** (cont.)

**Coal**

**(1) :** A new opencast coal site is commissioned at Parc Slip on the truncated Margam to Tondu line with an initial flow supplying coal to Westbury Cement Works:

    7C24,  Parc Slip - Westbury (L)               6B12,  Westbury   - Barry (E)

**(2) :** There is also a new supply of coal from Redcar Import Terminal to the cement works at Penyffordd and Clitheroe using MEA box wagons. The coal will alternatively be sourced through Hull and Immingham Docks plus, occasionally, a colliery in the South Yorkshire coalfield. The empty wagons combine at Healey Mills and work back to Teesside as one train.

    6M83,  Redcar   - Penyffordd (L)         6E41,  Penyffordd - Healey Mills (E)

    6M79,  Redcar   - Clitheroe (L)          6E73,  Clitheroe   - Healey Mills (E)

Unfortunately, although both cement works receive their supplies of coal by rail, all the output is despatched by road!

*Right* : Penyffordd cement works is situated on the Shotton to Wrexham line and in the sidings at the works, 08817 shunts MEA wagons after the arrival of the 6M83 service from Hull Docks. (PS)

*Below* : The services to Clitheroe necessitate a reversal at both Healey Mills and Hellifield in order to reach their destination.

Having already run round its train for the first time, 60100 *Boar of Badenoch* prepares to leave Healey Mills with loaded MEA's bound for Clitheroe, running on this occasion as 6Z98, the 01:30 Maltby - Clitheroe. (PS)

## SEPTEMBER

### Mail

Rail Express Systems (ReS) introduce their new class 325 mail units; 4-car sets, built at Derby and numbered 325001 - 325016. At the same time, a new Royal Mail distribution centre opens at Willesden and is the hub of all mail train movements in the UK. The first services are:

1A89, 15:43 Crewe - Willesden (325 unit)     1M65, 19:15  Plymouth- Willesden (class 47)

Further Royal Mail terminals will open in the next twelve months at Doncaster, Shieldmuir and Warrington, although, ironically, Royal Mail will sever its contract with EWS at the end of March 2004, bringing to an end 166 years of mail by rail!

*Top :* The 'hub' of the Royal Mail distribution centre is Willesden, which one can see is an expansive terminal with plenty of room for post handling. One of these new 325 units (325016) is stabled in a bay platform waiting its next turn of duty. (BM)

*Right :* One advantage the 325 units have over conventional mail vans is that they have sliding doors for easy access. This can be seen in this view of York trollies being loaded on platform 3, Carlisle, into one of the 325 units forming 1M90, the 12:52 Glasgow - Crewe mail. (DMc)

*Overleaf :* Sweeping down Shap bank on the WCML in Orton Moor cutting, two 325 units, headed by 325012, are in charge of 1M90, the 12:52 Glasgow Central  - Crewe mail. (MB)

## SEPTEMBER (cont.)

### Nuclear Waste

DRS begin running revenue earning trains between Sellafield and Barrow - in - Furness (nuclear flasks) and Drigg (low level radioactive waste). Traction for these services will be class 20/3 locomotives, in the Company's distinctive blue livery, followed by some former EPS class 37/6s.

*Top* : DRS successfully complete its first nuclear flask move on 19 September hauling four Magnox flasks from Sellafield. Here, 20301+20302 propel the flasks into the PNTL terminal at Ramsden Dock, Barrow. (DMc)

*Below* : The returning low level waste train, 7C21 Drigg to Sellafield, is seen alongside the delightful Cumbrian coastline at Seascale behind 08375. (DMc)

## SEPTEMBER (cont.)

### Coal

The sole colliery in North Wales closes - Point of Ayr - which used to supply MGR trainloads of coal to Fiddlers Ferry power station. The last train to leave the colliery was 6P62 to Fiddlers Ferry, hauled by 56133 *Crewe Locomotive Works*.

The colliery was situated on a reclaimed headland near the mouth of the River Dee estuary. Lord Mostyn, the owner of Mostyn colliery, instigated the first trial borings in 1865.

In its heyday in the 1950's, the colliery had a workforce in excess of 700 and produced more than 210,000 tonnes of coal annually.

*Right* : On the final day, the last working from Point of Ayr (6P62) is seen passing Glan-y-don, behind 56133 *Crewe Locomotive Works*. (RN)

### Minerals

Polybulk wagons start to appear on 6V23, the Hardendale - Margam lime train and will gradually replace the incumbent MGR-like 'covhop' wagons.

*Above* : Three of the new polybulk wagons can be seen along with conventional 'covhops' in the consist of 6V23 passing through the beautiful Lune Gorge behind Transrail-liveried 56010. (PJR)

# FREIGHTMASTER

## THE COMPLETE GUIDE TO BRITISH RAILFREIGHT OPERATIONS

Includes new Royal Mail Railnet workings

Winter 1996/97 Edition

Mark Rawlinson

### NOVEMBER : Petroleum

An announcement is made that Milford Haven oil refineries at Waterston and Robeston are to merge operations resulting in closure of the Waterston refinery.

### DECEMBER : Freight Operations

Loadhaul, Mainline and Transrail operating companies amalgamate under the EWS umbrella and EWS is announced as the preferred bidder for the last publicly owned railfreight company, Railfreight Distribution, incorporating Tinsley, Crewe International Electric Depot and Dollands Moor plus a substantial number of locomotives and rolling stock.

### Chemicals

DRS launch a new Nitric Acid service using NACCO tank wagons from Sandbach to Sellafield.

*Above* :DRS 20304+20305 pass Hartford in charge of 6P20, Sellafield - Sandbach empty acid tanks. (RN)

### 'Enterprise'

**(1) :** The Kronospan chipboard factory at Chirk reactivate a disused siding to receive timber from Scotland via an overnight Mossend to Warrington 'Enterprise' service.

**(2) :** Another new service brings in timber from North East Scotland to Hereford via Newport ADJ, which is later changed so that the timber is unloaded at Pontrilas, right outside the Timber Mill which requires it.

*Right* : This is the scene at the Kronospan factory at Chirk.

56120 has arrived with the 6J70 'trip' from Warrington with a trainload of timber from Arrochar and Beattock in OTA wagons.

Note the area clearly identified for MDF board. (PS)

*Above* : Any timber for Chirk conveyed on 6M63, Mossend - Warrington 'Enterprise' is tripped to the factory on 6J70, Arpley - Chirk, as we see here with Loadhaul liveried 60007 leaving Arpley Yard with loaded OTA wagons. (MB)

*Below* : ReS-liveried 47767 *St. Columbus* pauses by Pontrilas signalbox with 6M90, Newport ADJ - Bescot, 'Enterprise' which carries 7 OTAs of timber for Pontrilas plus a single Cargowaggon. (AK)

## JANUARY

### 'Enterprise'

All 'Enterprise' trips to Workington now use the docks rather than the station yard. The main traffic is for Iggesund Paperboard, comprising a new flow of paper pulp from Sheerness, plus timber and china clay. The reason for the switch is that the yard is nearer to the customer and has better road access.

*Right* : Freight for Iggesund; vans containing pulp and china clay tanks are shunted at Workington Docks by 37698, upon arrival with the 6C15 'Enterprise' trip from Carlisle. (DMc)

### Rolling Stock

Marcroft Engineering, Stoke, provide EWS with its first new wagons:

**Coal** : The first batch in a programme to convert 120 HEA coal hoppers to new MEA mineral box wagons (illustrated later) in EWS maroon & gold livery.

**Metals :** Sliding hood steel coil carrier No. 910303 is the first delivery in a conversion of 22 former BIA / BWA wagons, which will initially work out of Wolverhampton steel terminal.

*Above* : The new steel coil carriers are seen in Pangbourne cutting on the Great Western main line behind 37694 hauling 6O72, Wolverhampton Steel Terminal- Hoo Junction steel empties. (RN)

# FREIGHTMASTER

## THE COMPLETE GUIDE TO BRITISH RAILFREIGHT OPERATIONS

Spring
1997
Freight
Schedules

1st March
to
1st July

Mark Rawlinson

## MARCH : Coal

Imported coal starts flowing again from Hunterston Import Terminal for the first time since 1992 to English power stations, followed by flows to Longannet power station. The initial flow is:

6Z30, Hunterston - Drakelow (L)   6Z60, Drakelow - Hunterston (E)

### 'Enterprise'

**(1) :** EWS and Forth Ports initiate a return of railfreight services to Grangemouth Docks starting with two trains a week feeding into the 'Enterprise' network at Mossend. Materials handled at the port include, by way of example, blockboard and plywood from Tilbury.

*Right* : Ex-works in appearance, 37057 *Viking* stands at the head of a single VGA wagon and some Ferrywagons to form the first 'Enterprise' departure from the docks to Mossend. (IL)

**(2) :** Another new 'Enterprise' service starts running between Doncaster Railport and Harwich to connect with the Stena Ferry to Zeebrugge using FKA container flats but, after a year or so of operating, the service is withdrawn due to inadequate loadings. However, this service does make a comeback in 2004 in the guise of 6L55, Wakefield - Felixstowe.

The Harwich 'Enterprise' runs as:

6L79, Doncaster Railport - Harwich   6E76, Harwich - Doncaster

*Above* : If this view was a typical daily payload, then 6L79 / 6E76 would have almost certainly survived. On the outskirts of Peterborough, a pair of class 37's (37116 *Sister Dora* leading) pass Holme Load with 6L79 ex - Doncaster. (JR)

**MARCH** (cont.)

### Freight Operations

Freight is banned on the Tay bridge in Scotland and means that all freight services running between Edinburgh and Aberdeen must be rerouted via Perth.

### Locomotives

MendipRail hire out two class 59 locomotives to EWS to work the iron ore tipplers between Port Talbot Docks and Llanwern steelworks.

*Above* : Mendip Rail 59004 *Paul A Hammond* passes Pengam freightliner terminal, Cardiff, with a rake of empty Iron ore tipplers forming 6B60, Llanwern - Port Talbot. In the terminal, 47301 is stabled for 4L56 to Felixstowe and 47337 + 47150 marshal containers for the 4S81 service to Coatbridge. Of note, is that the freightliner terminal would close in February 2001 and be replaced by a new terminal at Wentloog, about a mile or so further east. (MB)

**MARCH** (cont.) **: Construction Materials**

**(1) :** The start of sea defence work at Minehead sees a new flow of stone and boulders (rock armour to be precise!) from the Mendips using turbot wagons. As Minehead is not connected to the main rail network, permission has been granted for the trains to travel over the lines of the West Somerset Railway in order to reach the destination and so preserve a continuous journey by rail. Two photographs are included to illustrate this unique flow, which is:

8C25, Merehead - Minehead (L)  7C26, Minehead - Merehead (E)

*Opposite Page* : 8C25 on the West Somerset Railway. En-route to Minehead, 37332 (*top left*) hauls a rake of 14 YCV Turbot wagons at Roebuck Farm while, at the destination, 37718 (*bottom left*) shunts 8C25 at Minehead station amidst a fine array of GWR railwayana. (Both AK)

*Right* : 'Forticrete' concrete slabs are shown to good effect in the consist of a 'Jumbo' MendipRail aggregate service seen heading away from the camera past the 'Berks & Hants' canal at Little Bedwyn. The train in view is the 7A17, Merehead to Acton, headed by 59004 *Paul A. Hammond*. (AK)

*Bottom* : During unloading, we see 59001 *Yeoman Endeavour* at Exeter Riverside yard having arrived from the Mendips, forming 7Z85, ex- Merehead. It is interesting to note that during this project, which would take 2½ years to complete, some 691 trains would run conveying over 820,000 tonnes of stone! (DM)

**(2) :** 'Forticrete' concrete slabs are now moved by rail to Foster Yeoman's terminal at Acton Yard on the rear of Merehead - Acton trains, usually on 7A17, Merehead - Acton yard

**(3) :** Another contract sees the movement of roadstone from Merehead to an unloading facility at Exeter Riverside yard for use on the A30 Honiton By-Pass involving two train services:

7Z83, Merehead - Exeter Riverside (L)  7Z84, Exeter - Merehead (E)
7Z85, Merehead - Exeter (L)  7Z86, Exeter - Merehead (E)

## APRIL

### Mail

Doncaster Railnet Terminal, situated on the former Decoy Yard on the downside of the ECML, opens for business and is the end of mail handling at Doncaster, Leeds and Sheffield stations.

*Right* : The terminal is a two line platform and 47736 *Cambridge Traction and Rolling Stock Depot* waits to depart with 1V64, the 14:03 Low Fell - Plymouth mail. Several lines still remain in the yard to cater for MGR coal traffic to/from the Yorkshire and Nottinghamshire coalfields. (CB)

## MAY : Freightliner / Intermodal

Two new terminals open for business this month:

**(1)** : Daventry International Rail Freight Terminal (acronym DRIFT). Situated adjacent to Jct. 18 of the M1, Daventry will be used for Intermodal traffic to Europe via the Channel Tunnel. It is the largest intermodal terminal to open in the UK but, unfortunately, the location does not lend itself to photographic opportunities.

**(2)** : Purfleet. This terminal will see a new service linking Purfleet and Zeebrugge, with 5 daily sailings in conjunction with Cobelfret the Belgian shipper; all freightliner traffic will be tripped to Purfleet from Tilbury. Class 47 (No. 47114) is named *Freightlinerbulk* in two tone green livery and Freightliner branding to market the Company's bulk powder and liquid traffic.

*Above* : The distinctive 47114 is seen at South Bank, Teesside, in charge of 4M21, Wilton - Crewe freightliner; a suitable working for this locomotive conveying bulk chemicals from the ICI plant at Wilton. (AK)

## JUNE : Intermodal

The 30th.of this month sees the start of a unique daily trial to transport milk from Penrith to Cricklewood for Milk Marque, a company who are responsible for selling over 50% of the UK's milk. The train, known as the 'Milkliner', will comprise 2 x DRS class 20s and Tiphook 'Piggyback' wagons, which will transport the actual milk lorry, wheels and all! Although this trial is not a success, we will see 'Piggyback' again with operations by Parcelforce and Blue Circle Cement.

*Above* : Descending Grayrigg at Docker, 20303 (complete with 'Milkliner 2000' commemorative headboard) double-heads 20304, the locomotives entrusted to work 4Z58, the 12:53 Penrith - Cricklewood 'Milkliner'. (PJR)

*Below* : On the first day of operation, 20304 + 20301 run round the train in Penrith yard prior to departure with 4Z58, the 12:53 service to Cricklewood. Rather than take on a full milk tanker, the first rail load was an empty one which was then filled by two smaller road tankers. (DMc)

# *FREIGHTMASTER*

## THE COMPLETE GUIDE TO BRITISH RAILFREIGHT OPERATIONS

**NEW** Freight Schedules for Summer/Autumn 1997

1st July to 1st November

Mark Rawlinson

## JULY

### Petrochemicals

British Petroleum (BP) despatch the 3,000th trainload of Liquefied Petroleum Gas (LPG) from their loading point at Furzebrook, near Wareham, to Hallen Marsh, Avonmouth.

*Right* : This is the scene at the loading point at Furzebrook as 60039 shunts empty 4-wheel tank wagons after arriving with 6W53 from Eastleigh. The loaded tanks of Propane and Butane will eventually depart as the 6V29 service to Hallen Marsh. (CB)

### Metals

EWS marks a close association with one of its biggest customers, British Steel, by naming two class 60 locomotives at Scunthorpe steelworks; 60006 *Scunthorpe Ironmaster* and 60033 *Tees Steel Express. Also,* Brush Traction outshop the two locomotives in British Steel's bright blue house colour.

*Right* : Appropriately, 60006 passes some fine semaphores at Wrawby Junction, Barnetby, heading 6T24, Immingham - Scunthorpe iron ore tipplers. (RN)

### Freightliner / Intermodal

Hams Hall freight terminal, operated by American company Parsec, opens for business and to mark the occasion, 47312 is named *Parsec of Europe* and works the first train out of the terminal, 4P55 to Wembley.

*Right* : This is the terminal at Hams Hall with 08453 in view at the head of a train of containers. (PS)

*Below* : Having left the main line at Whitacre Junction, 47326 S*altley Depot* .... + 47362 arrive at Hams Hall with 4P12 intermodal from Wembley. (RN)

## JULY (cont.) 'Enterprise'

Whilst waiting for EEC clearance for the sale of RfD to EWS, EWS completely revamp the 'Enterprise' wagonload network by merging 'Enterprise' and 'Connectrail' and incorporating MoD traffic at the same time. However, until the takeover takes place, services to continental Europe together with certain connecting services to & from London will remain operated by RfD under the 'Connectrail' banner.

As a consequence, three daily 90-hauled services from Wembley are introduced which include two trains to the West Midlands and a  new "Gold Star' 75mph service to Scotland:

    4S68, Wembley - Mossend                4M78, Mossend - Wembley

In addition, there is a daily diesel-hauled trunk service linking Kent and Scotland:

    6S75, Sheerness to Mossend

A further example of the new operations sees the introduction of another long distance trunk 'Enterprise' service between the South Coast and Carlisle carrying MoD stores (for Eastriggs and Longtown) plus 'Enterprise' traffic to/from Quidhampton and Workington. Of note, is that MoD traffic always takes priority! The new service runs as:

    6M18, Eastleigh - Carlisle

The main 'Enterprise' hubs at present are listed below with Doncaster joining the system later in order to remove the need of Warrington dealing with east coast traffic.

| | | | |
|---|---|---|---|
| - Bescot | - Carlisle | - Eastleigh | - Newport |
| - Mossend | - Warrington | - Wembley | - Willesden |

From these 'hubs', trip workings connect to/from the 'Enterprise' trunk services (*see page 11*) to local terminals/sidings (*See map opposite*) conveying a range of products, such as:

| | | | |
|---|---|---|---|
| Bloxwich | : Steel | Cameron Bridge | : Carbon Dioxide |
| Eastriggs | : MoD stores | Ely | : General goods |
| Neasden | : Bottled water | Runcorn | : Salt |
| Quidhampton | : Calcium Carbonate | Taynuilt | : Timber |

*Above* : One of the new 'Enterprise' services (6S75) is about to pass through Milton Keynes station behind 'grid' 56101 *Mutual Improvement* with a varied consist including four wagons of steel wire. (NG)

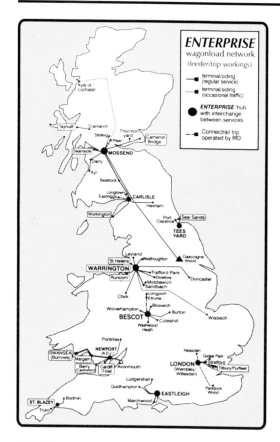

*Above* : This is a typical 'Enterprise' trip; 6F81, Runcorn Folly Lane - Arpley, conveying industrial salt bound for Scotland. The train is hauled by 31110 and is passing Arpley Junction. (MB)

*Left* : Map showing 'Enterprise' trips. (MR)

*Above* : This is the new 6M18, Eastleigh to Carlisle 'Enterprise' service, which replaces the previous Didcot to Crewe (6M29) and Crewe to Carlisle (6C61) MoD trains. The train is seen passing Hinksey Yard on the southern approach to Oxford with 47362 in charge of a consist of MoD stores and departmental wagons. (RN)

## JULY (cont.) Construction Materials

**(1) :** Flyash, a by-product from coal burning power stations, is used in the manufacture of cement and concrete and a new flow starts between Longannet power station to Westbury cement works.

**(2) :** Expansion at Manchester Airport sees stone being brought in by rail on a dedicated service for the building of a second runway:

 6H05, Tunstead - Manchester Airport (L)     6H04, Manchester Airport - Tunstead (E)

*Above* : With Dunimarle Castle punctuating the tree-line, 56067 approaches Culross shortly after leaving Longannet with loaded flyash bound for Westbury cement works, which will arrive via Mossend and Newport ADJ. (IL)

*Below* : The Manchester Airport stone trains traverse the 'freight only' line between Hazel Grove H. L. Junction and Northenden Junction, on which we see 60089 *Arcuil* passing Cheadle Heath, with a combination of easily recognisable Tiphook and RMC bogie hopper wagons forming 6H05 for Manchester Airport. (PS)

**(3) :** The Summer continues to be a busy period for the construction industry with work starting on the Puddletown by-pass on the A35 near Dorchester. Stone is being brought in from the Mendips to a temporary terminal at Hamworthy.

7O39, Merehead - Hamworthy (L)

7V89, Hamworthy - Merehead (E)

*Right* : Sporting a cast metal BR emblem and Petroleum sector decals, 37708 is about to rejoin the main line at Hamworthy with 7V89, Hamworthy - Merehead stone empties which will travel via Poole, Eastleigh, Salisbury and Westbury. (DM)

## SEPTEMBER

### Petroleum

Freight traffic resumes on the West Drayton to Colnbrook branch, albeit only one service of bogie tanks conveying petroleum for Heathrow Airport:

6A14, Robeston - Colnbrook (L)          6B23, Colnbrook - Robeston (E)

### Intermodal

Superdrug start using rail to move its products from Wakefield to Scotland (Mossend) using ferrywagons loaded at Wakefield Cobra railfreight terminal.

This is an interesting development as it marks an increase in the use of rail by large retail groups to transport their goods throughout the UK. Later, as we shall see in this review, retailers such as ASDA, Argos, B & Q, and Safeway will also follow suit.

### Construction Materials

**(1) :** Following the Manchester Airport project, which started in July, another construction project begins in Greater Manchester this month with the extension of the M63 motorway. Redland will convey stone to a temporary terminal at Ashburys using MEA box wagons:

6H50, Dowlow - Ashburys (L)          6H51, Ashburys - Dowlow (E)

**(2) :** EWS combine forces with MendipRail to provide regular supplies of stone for the construction of a new storage & distribution facility for Honda at Avonmouth. Up to 5 trains a day will run using 102-tonne bogie box wagons.

*Right* : Two class 37 locomotives, sporting Mainline and EWS liveries, provide a fine sight as they pass Narroways Hill Junction, Bristol, which gives access to Severn Beach. The train engines are 37219 + 37886 hauling a rake of 16 PTA / PHA / JYA wagons forming 7Z88, the 15:30 Whatley - Rockingham Road Bridge. (AK)

**SEPTEMBER** (cont.)

### Domestic Waste

After several years absence the Greater Manchester Council (GMC) waste trains ('Binliners') return to the railway network running from Bredbury and Northenden Refuse Transfer Stations (RTS) to a landfill site at Roxby Gullet, near Scunthorpe. Of particular interest is the routing of these trains which follow a 'figure of eight'; the Bredbury train is routed out via Diggle and returns via the Hope Valley, while the Northenden train does the opposite.

The services are:

| | | |
|---|---|---|
| 6E06, | Bredbury | - Roxby (L) |
| 6E05, | Northenden | - Roxby (L) |

| | | |
|---|---|---|
| 6M06, | Roxby | - Bredbury (E) |
| 6M05, | Roxby | - Northenden (E) |

*Right* : A busy scene at Frodingham, Scunthorpe. As 56060 slows for a reversal with 7C79, the 16:33 Immingham - Scunthorpe loaded MGR, 60018 proceeds along the slow line with 6M06 empty 'binliner' bound for Bredbury. The landfill site at Roxby is on a single track line, accessed from Trent Junction, which is visible to the left of the last MGR wagon of 7C79. (MB)

*Below* : An interesting composition showing the layout at Northenden Junction. The main line links Stockport and Altrincham while the single track leads to Hazel Grove H. L. Junction.

The Refuse Transfer Station is situated on the right, where 56099 *Fiddlers Ferry Power Station* reverses 6M05 from Roxby into the terminal. (PS)

*Above* : On the Roxby Gullet branch ...... 60076 passes Dragonby on a cold Winter's morning with 6M05, Roxby - Northenden empty GMC containers; a service which along with the Bredbury train is a solid class 56/60 turn. (CB)

*Below* : At the Landfill site, 60052 prepares to leave with 6M05 to Northenden. (PS)

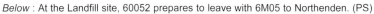

## OCTOBER

### Freightliner

Quite a month for Freightliner ....

**(1)** : This month is the 25th anniversary of freightliner operations at Southampton Docks following the building of the Maritime terminal in 1972; 47334 is named *P & O Nedlloyd* to mark the 25 year partnership between the shipping line, its predecessor and Freightliner.

*Right* : The newly named 47334 *P & O Nedlloyd* passes South Bank, Middlesbrough, in charge of 4N52, Tees Yard - Wilton freightliner; Middlesbrough transporter bridge is visible in the background. (PJR)

**(2)** : Freightliner make a welcome return to the Port of Hull after 10 years with a new service linking Hull and Manchester, using P & O North Sea Ferries to Rotterdam and Zeebrugge. This service also means the return of freightliner traffic to the Standedge trans-pennine route:

4E59,  Trafford Park - Hull                    4M09,  Hull        - Crewe Basford Hall

**(3)** : A new freight flow begins involving the movement of containerised Nylon Polymer from Wilton (Teesside) to Doncaster in distinctive IBC containers:

4D87,  Wilton         - Doncaster Railport      4N88,  Doncaster - Wilton

*Above* : On the ECML, with an Aire Valley power station visible on the horizon, 47376 passes Burn heading the Nylon Polymer container service back to Wilton, running on this occasion as 4N90, Doncaster - Tees Yard. (RN)

**OCTOBER** (cont.)

### Mail

Two new Royal Mail terminals open at Shieldmuir and Warrington, thus ending mail handling at Glasgow Central and Crewe, Liverpool, Manchester, Preston, respectively.

### Metals

**(1)** : The Associated British Port of Hull features the country's first fully enclosed steel handling facility; a structure built over the former No.2 dry dock at King George Dock which can accommodate ships upto 6,000 tonnes and offers direct transfer to rail using overhead gantry cranes. To commemorate the occasion, 56087 is aptly named *Port of Hull*.

Any steel is moved to/from Hull on the daily 'Enterprise' service:

6D51, Doncaster  - Hull            6D54,  Hull      - Doncaster

**(2)** : EWS secure a new contract to move scrap metal from scrapyards at Handsworth and Swindon to Liverpool Alexandra Dock for European Metals.

6F73,  Handsworth - Liverpool (L)

6M73,  Swindon    - Liverpool (L)        6V72,  Liverpool - Swindon (E)

**(3)** : Also this month ..... some good news is the return of freight traffic to the Sleaford - Skegness line with the movement of steel from Boston Docks to the West Midlands using sliding hood steel carriers. Initially, the flow is a very stop/start affair and it is not until the following year before regular services begin in earnest. Furthermore, these services run as specials ('Z') and it is not until 1999 that they are allocated timetabled reporting numbers:

6M01,  Boston     - Toton (L)         6M04,  Toton     - Round Oak (L)

6M05,  Round Oak - Toton (E)        6E02,  Toton     - Boston (E)

*Above* : On the seldom photographed Nottingham - Sleaford line, 56101 *Mutual Improvement* passes the signalbox at Ancaster station with covered empty steel containers forming 6Z92, Toton - Boston Docks. (CB)

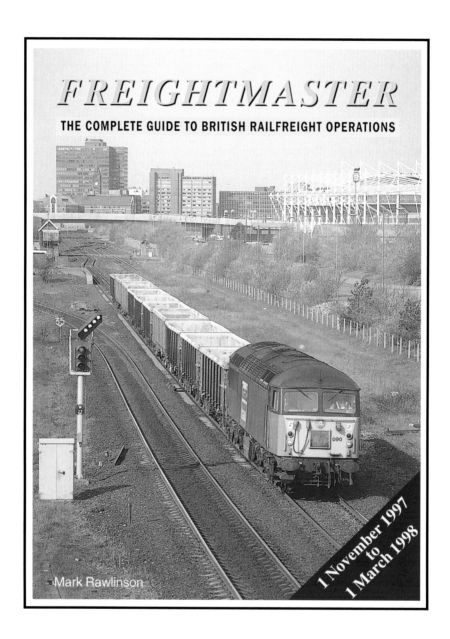

# FREIGHTMASTER

**THE COMPLETE GUIDE TO BRITISH RAILFREIGHT OPERATIONS**

Mark Rawlinson

1 November 1997
to
1 March 1998

## NOVEMBER : Coal

Start of a new flow of coal from a brand new coal terminal at Avonmouth to Rugby cement works using MEA box wagons; the coal can also be sourced from Newport Docks.

6M17,  Avonmouth -  Rugby (L)

6V87,  Rugby        -  Didcot Yard (E)        6B88,  Didcot - Avonmouth (E)

*Previous Page* : The railway lines at Patchway Tunnel, Bristol, are at different levels with the southbound line being at a lower level, on which 37718 heads 6M17, Newport Docks - Rugby, having emerged from the south portal of Patchway Tunnel with MEA wagons loaded with coal. (MB)

### Freight Operations - RfD & EWS

**(1)** : Following the sale of RfD to EWS, the respective freight services are amalgamated. EWS incorporate Tinsley, Crewe Electric depot and Dollands Moor plus a substantial number of locomotives and rolling stock. The last RfD train is 4M63, Dollands Moor - Wembley.

*Right* : One such service is 4M72, Mossend - Wembley intermodal, seen at Mill Meece interestingly hauled by 87101 *Stephenson*. (RN)

**(2)** : One of RfD's last acts was to open an international freight terminal at Tilbury, sited on the former Tilbury Riverside station area. The first commercial train leaves on the opening day (24/11/97) carrying goods for Spain, hauled by 47293 which had been named *Transfesa*.

*Above* : This picture shows the layout of the new Tilbury freight terminal on the opening day, where 47293 *Transfesa* heads a train of 5 containers bound for Spain alongside RFS-liveried 08 shunter No. 08764. (BM)

## JANUARY

### Minerals

End of an era .... PGA hoppers start work on the Tunstead - Northwich limestone circuit and replace the 1930s built vacuum braked PHV ex-ICI bogie limestone hoppers for Brunner Mond; the last vacuum brake freight operation on the rail network! The replacement wagons are a fleet of 112, previously stored, PGA hoppers with the old ARC and Yeoman markings obliterated.

*Above Left* : A reminder of the old style wagons in service on the Northwich to Altrincham line, with 37509+37518 passing Hale with with 7F52, Tunstead - Northwich, loaded hoppers. (RN)

*Above Right* : A close up of one of these ex-ICI vacuum brake bogie hoppers - BLI 19055 at Winnington. (PS)

### Petroleum

End of oil traffic over Shap!......... Shell UK decide to scale down petroleum operations at its Stanlow refinery, Ellesmere Port, and means the end of regular oil traffic between Stanlow and Jarrow; the only oil traffic to travel over the WCML between Preston and Carlisle. Jarrow now receives oil from Lindsey instead.

*Above* : On a bright Spring day, EWS-liveried 60047 sweeps down Shap and passes through Orton Mere cutting, near Greenholme, with the returning petroleum empties (6M19) from Jarrow bound for Stanlow. (MB)

# FREIGHTMASTER

## THE COMPLETE GUIDE TO BRITISH RAILFREIGHT OPERATIONS

1 March 1998
to
1 July 1998

Mark Rawlinson

## MARCH

### Minerals

Due to the failure of the desulphurisation plant at Drax power station, Gypsum is being imported into the UK to the British Gypsum plant at Kirkby Thore, Newbiggin, through Hunterston and, alternatively, Hartlepool Docks. The trains run as specials and are both illustrated here.

With the Lowther Hills in the background, 60028 *John Flamsteed (Above)* passes Closeburn on the ex- Glasgow & South Western main line with 6Z32, the 14:32 Hunterston - Newbiggin containerised Gypsum. Meanwhile, in the delightful Tyne valley near Hexham, 56096 (*Below*) is seen heading another train of Gypsum en-route to Kirkby Thore forming 6Z93, the 10:45 Hartlepool Docks - Newbigginn. (both PJR)

### APRIL

### Coal

EWS take over National Power's rail operation using the distinctive blue liveried locomotives and bogie hoppers. Eventually, the locomotives will be repainted in standard EWS colours and the wagons will be transferred to the Liverpool Gladstone Dock - Fiddlers Ferry coal circuit.

### Locomotives

The first new locomotive ordered by EWS arrives at Immingham on April 18th. - the General Motors built class 66, No. 66001, a tangible sign of the Company's £500 million investment programme in new locomotives and rolling stock. The loco. had been transported across the Atlantic from Albany, New York, in the hold of the Dutch-registered MV *Fairload*.

The class will ultimately total 250 and have a virtual monopoly on freight services throughout the UK; christened 'sheds' by rail enthusiasts they will become the 'universal' freight engine, thus removing any problems with traction knowledge among train crews; a position which probably should have happened when steam finished way back in 1968!

*Right* : A dismal day greets photographers, keen to record the first class 66 hauled service in the UK for posterity. 66001 (with 56044 tucked inside 'just in case') passes Coedkernew heading 6B62, Grange Sidings - Llanwern loaded MGR. (DM)

*Below* : This was to become a familiar sight at Newport Docks during the next couple of years, the unloading of new class 66 locomotives.

Not the first to arrive, but the last batch ...... 66240-66250 wait to leave Newport Docks having been unloaded from the hold of MV *Fairload* earlier in the day. The Dutch-registered 'Jumboship' is specifically designed for moving heavy cargo and is equipped with integral 250-tonnes cranes. (AK)

## JUNE : 'Enterprise'

A new freight facility opens at the Kyle of Lochalsh to handle traffic for the Western Isles. To inaugurate the new facility, 37684 *Peak National Park* works in a special freight.

At the Kyle, 37684 *(Right)* arrives with 6Z46, the 06:35 Inverness - Kyle of Lochalsh 'Enterprise' service, formed mainly of empty OTA timber wagons. Later that day, the class 37 *(below)* is about to break the tartan ribbon to open the new freight facility, which is adjacent to Kyle of Lochalsh station. (both PJR)

## Intermodal

Parcelforce operate the first timetabled 'piggyback' wagon service between London and Glasgow with the actual lorry container (wheels and all) being carried by rail. The service is:

4S99, Willesden - Mossend                    4M75, Mossend - Willesden

*Above* : This photograph shows the 'piggyback' operation as 86243 heads south along the WCML near Soulbury, south of Bletchley, heading 4M75, Mossend - Willesden; note, the additional intermodal traffic on the rear of the train! (NG)

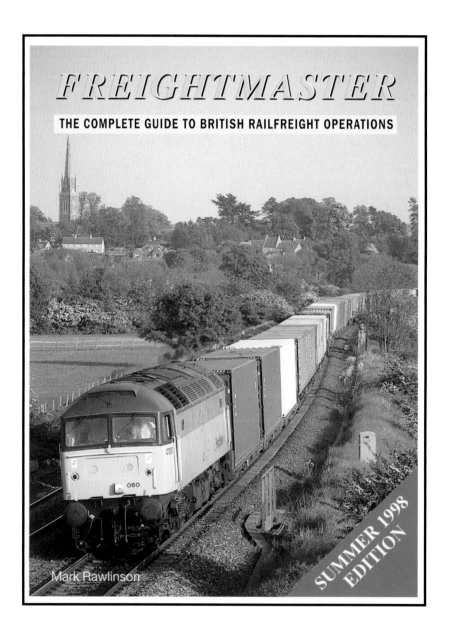

# FREIGHTMASTER

## THE COMPLETE GUIDE TO BRITISH RAILFREIGHT OPERATIONS

060

Mark Rawlinson

SUMMER 1998 EDITION

## JULY

### Locomotives

**(1) :** Freightliner unveil their new class 57 locomotive (57001, ex-47356) rebuilt with a General Motors 2,500hp engine and is the first of a dozen members in the class, all class 47 rebuilds. The new 57001 sports Freightliner's new corporate livery of green with yellow branding which will be adopted for use on the Company's fleet of class 86/6 and later class 66/5 locomotives.

**(2) :** Having been confined to Wembley - Dollands Moor services since first being introduced, the class 92 locomotives are finally breaking out into new territory by working 'Enterprise' services over the northern stretches of the WCML between Crewe / Warrington and Mossend.

*Right* : Somewhat reminiscent of the 'Speedlink' era, 92007 *Schubert* hauls a variety of wagons on the climb to Shap summit, near Harrisons Quarry, forming 6O12, Mossend - Eastleigh 'Enterprise'.

The consist includes two china clay slurry tanks, plus two distinctive green liveried bogie tank wagons from the Dalston - Grangemouth petroleum circuit and some OTA wagons loaded with logs. (DMc)

*Below* : The latest edition to the Freightliner fleet, 57001 *Freightliner Pioneer*, is seen hauling a fully loaded 4O26, Crewe - Southampton freightliner past Fenny Compton on the Didcot - Birmingham main line.

These locomotives will replace the fleet of ageing class 47s on the non-electrified sections of the freightliner network. (AK)

## AUGUST : Nuclear Waste

DRS take over responsibility from EWS of all movements of spent nuclear fuel from nuclear power stations in the UK to Sellafield, but it will be a further six months until all services are operated by DRS. The last ever flask working operated by EWS was to Berkeley nuclear power station and, on the occasion of the last working, the crossover from the 'down' main line to the branch at Berkeley Road Junction was out of use. So, the train had to travel to Stoke Gifford to reverse and then back up to the junction where another reversal was required to get onto the branch. For operating ease, the train was top 'n' tailed by 37375 and 37689.

*Top* : Against a skyline dominated by electricity pylons, 20308 + 37609 haul 7Z81, the 13:03 Hartlepool - Sellafield nuclear flasks away from the power station to join the main line at Seaton Snook Junction. (PJR)

*Right* : Operationally, all nuclear flask services run with more than a single locomotive to work the train. The reason for this is 'safety in numbers' in case of failure and to move locomotives into position to work other DRS services.

A trio of 37s (37218, 37059, 37612) approach Parton on the Cumbrian coast line with 6C22, Carlisle - Sellafield. The train has just left the single line section at Lowca, singled to aid protection from the elements. Note the rock armour giving protection from the sea and the small wall to guard against landslip is also visible. (DMc)

## AUGUST (cont.)

### Coal

An opencast coal site opens at Broomhills, south east of Ayr. Fairly uniquely, operations necessitate the train having a brake van because of the long propelling movement off the mainline to the loading point over two level crossings!

*Right* : Romanian built 56004, complete with brake van at the rear, propels 6Z71, the 14:52 Falkland Yard - Broomhills down the branch to the loading point. (AK)

### Construction Materials

**(1)** : A new flow this month sees the movement of Ground Granulated Blast Furnace Slag (GGBFS) from Llanwern steelworks to Cardiff Docks for use in the construction of a waste Water Treatment Works by Laing. Several trains run each day as 'specials' using two trainsets, formed of 35 MEA box wagons capable of carrying 1,600 tonnes, hauled by the unique class 37/9 locomotives. During February, GGBFS also started to be moved from Port Talbot to Godstone in connection with construction work at Gatwick Airport.

**(2)** : Sea defence traffic from Merehead to Southampton Eastern Docks starts for onward movement to Ventnor, Isle of Wight, using converted MHA wagons.

**(3)** : Southern water's flood relief scheme for Hastings involves the removal of 130,000 tonnes of spoil. It is carried by conveyor to a siding near the station where it is loaded into bogie box wagons and transported to the ARC quarry at Allington.

*Above* : Passing an orchard in the Garden of England (Kent), 58014 heads 7H80, the 10:10 Hastings - Allington spoil train at Five Oak Green near Paddock Wood. (BM)

### OCTOBER

### Construction Materials

One of the biggest infrastructure projects begins this month with the construction of the Cross Channel Rail Link (CTRL) linking a new Eurostar terminal at London St. Pancras, with Paris. The initial work involves the construction of a high speed railway line through the Kent countryside with aggregate for the project brought in from the Mendips to an unloading terminal at Sevington.

### Metals

New EWS telescopic steel coil carrying wagons, built at Thrall Europa, York, enter service.

*Right* : A close up of a new wagon (BYA 966208) at Wakefield. (PS)

*Below* : The new telescopic wagons make up the majority of wagons in the consist of 6V75, Dee Marsh - Margam, headed by 60002 *Freight Transport Association* seen passing Newport ADJ. Also in view are two class 66 locomotives, plus 60094+60067 ready to leave with 6M17, Newport ADJ - Wembley intermodal. (MB)

## OCTOBER (cont.)

### Chemicals

As part of the 'Enterprise' system, EWS start a new service linking Teesport and the Port of Workingon involving the movement of containerised chemicals for Hoyer.

The containers are 'tripped' from Workington Docks, thence:

6E62, Carlisle   - Tees Dock

6M57, Tees Dock - Carlisle

The service proves a success and will eventually run 7 days a week! Interestingly, the (MO) train starts back at Workington as 6E79 and on a Saturday, 6E62 terminates at Tees Yard before going forward to Tees Dock as 6N52 on Sunday.

*Right* : With the famous Middlesbrough transporter bridge dominating the skyline, 56081 approaches Tees Yard with the empty containers forming 6M57, (Sun) Tees Dock - Carlisle. (MB)

## NOVEMBER

### Freightliner / Intermodal

A new terminal (O'Connors) opens at Ditton, Widnes, on the site of the old BOC plant, and will ostensibly handle Freightliner traffic.

A second terminal (operated by AHC) will open the following year, principally handling EWS Intermodal traffic.

These terminals are a welcome addition to the freight scene around Merseyside and will eventually handle direct trains to destinations such as Felixstowe, Purfleet, Southampton Western Docks and Thamesport (Grain).

*Right* : The layout of the O'Connors terminal is well illustrated in this general view of the yard, which has three reception lines and is situated at a lower level than the WCML in the background.

A crane manoeuvres a container into position as 47370 prepares to depart with 4F02, Ditton - Garston. Note, the white tanks in the distance which convey chemicals. (PS)

# FREIGHTMASTER

Winter
Edition
1998/99

Mark Rawlinson

**THE COMPLETE GUIDE TO BRITISH RAILFREIGHT OPERATIONS**

## DECEMBER : Minerals

For the first time in over 20 years, freight traffic returns to East Leake (Hotchley Hill) on the former Great Central Railway north of Loughborough and the flow is containerised Gypsum. The service runs as a special until 2001 when the trains are allocated WTT reporting numbers:

6M58, Drax - East Leake (L)                    6E76, East Leake - Knottingley (E)

*Above* : At East Leake, 66219 prepares to depart with empty Gypsum containers forming the 6E76 service to Milford Junction which, along with Sudforth Lane, are alternative destinations to Knottingley. (PS)

## JANUARY 1999

### Infrastructure

A review of infrastructure train requirements results in the formation of engineers trains being done at a handful of 'Local Distribution Centres' (LDC), most of which have 'virtual quarries' and 'virtual tips' to stockpile ballast & spoil, respectively. A map showing these is shown overleaf.

This method of working is more efficient and reduces unnecessary train movements during the week; it has also resulted in the abolition of most of the unpredictable 'target' workings, such as Bescot T70, T90 and L52 trips, which have all become timetabled services.

*Right* : This is the Local Distribution Centre at Newport Alexandra Dock Junction (ADJ) and is fairly typical of the other sites around the country.

As can be seen here, the LDC is located adjacent to the main ADJ yard, separated by the lines which give access to Newport Docks.

In this view, 09203 *Wrighty* (unofficial name!) shunts an assortment of wagons of ballast, probably sourced from Machen Quarry.

Note, the large stockpile of ballast and a stack of concrete sleepers. (AK)

**JANUARY** (cont.)

**Infrastructure**

The major LDCs are strategically located around the country at:

| | | | |
|---|---|---|---|
| Bescot | Carnforth | Doncaster | Eastleigh |
| Guide Bridge | Hinksey | Hoo Junction | Millerhill |
| Mossend | Newport ADJ | Peterborough | Rugby |
| Temple Mills | Toton | Tyne Yard | Westbury |

*Below* : The map shows these locations along with details of the infrastructure network. (MR)

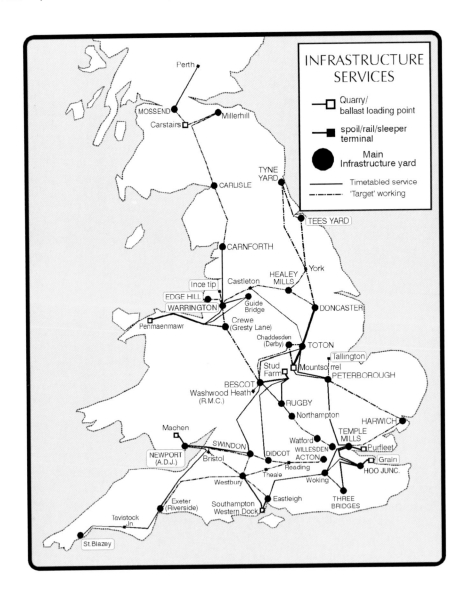

# FREIGHTMASTER

## THE COMPLETE GUIDE TO BRITISH RAILFREIGHT OPERATIONS

LATEST CLASS 66 WORKINGS

SPRING 1999 EDITION

Mark Rawlinson

## MARCH : Minerals

This month sees the 10th. anniversary of the longest freight flow in the country, the transportation of china clay slurry between Cornwall and Scotland for use in the paper industry.

The train was nicknamed the 'Silver Bullet' because of the highly polished tank wagons but, as the years went by, the wagons soon became a grimy shade of grey due to a lack of polishing.

Originally, the service (6S55 / 6V41) was a through working, but now runs via Newport ADJ and is recoded accordingly.

Before and after ...

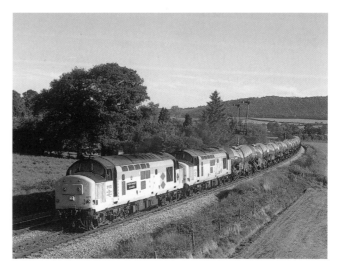

*Top Right* : Regular cleaning & polishing finished about 1992 / 93 but when the tanks were cleaned they positively gleaned as we see here as 37672 *Freight Transport Association* + 37674 head 6S55, Burngullow - Irvine, passing Cheney Longville near Craven Arms. (RN)

*Right* : Later, the tanks look distinctively drab as 37670 *St. Blazey* + 37669 approach Teignmouth with 6S55, which happened to be the last day (22/7/95) of rostered class 37 traction for this train, suitably adorned with commemorative headboard. (DM)

## JUNE : Petrochemicals

A freight casualty ....

    6V26, Burn Naze - Barry Docks (L)

    6M45, Barry Docks - Burn Naze (E)

.... the end of Vinyl Chloride Monomer between Burn Naze and Barry Docks in the distinctive white bogie tanks with orange stripe.

*Right* : Initially, only 08's were allowed down the docks, 'tripping' the wagons up to Cadoxton where the mainline engine would take over. Mainline engines were subsequently allowed down the docks, starting with RfD 47's, as seen here with 47287 waiting to depart with 6M45. (AK)

## Channel Tunnel

It only seems like yesterday, but 5 years have elapsed since the commencement of Channel Tunnel freight operations and, to commemorate the 5th. anniversary, 92001 *Victor Hugo* works a train of Rover cars through the tunnel - the first EWS-liveried locomotive in France!

**JUNE** (cont.)

### Construction Materials

A new EWS cement service for Blue Circle between Earles Sidings, Hope, and Moorswater commences and is a welcome return of traffic to the former china clay branch line.

6V91, Earles - Moorswater

The empties are then tripped to St. Blazey, thence returning to the Peak District as:

6M91, St. Blazey - Earles.

*Right* : 37513 propels the loaded cement tanks along the branch towards the new cement distribution depot at Moorswater. (DM)

*Above* : China clay production ceased at Moorswater in June 1997 and this new flow is a pleasing return to the former works. At the depot itself, 37676 has arrived with 6V91 from Earles. Long after the introduction of class 66s, 37's were still used in Devon and Cornwall due to restricted clearances within the works. (AK)

# FREIGHTMASTER

## THE COMPLETE GUIDE TO BRITISH RAILFREIGHT OPERATIONS

Revised "ENTERPRISE" Schedules

58014

SUMMER 1999 EDITION

Mark Rawlinson

## JULY

### Locomotives

Freightliner take delivery of 66501, the first of a substantial number of 66/5 locomotives, which will replace their ageing fleet of 47s.

The new locomotive arrived at Newport Docks along with 66502 and, after unloading and commissioning, were moved to Pengam freightliner terminal, Cardiff. The pair then worked 4L56, Pengam - Ipswich Yard freightliner.

*Right* : This illustration shows the unloading of a subsequent batch of locomotives at Newport Docks with 66506 and 66510 in view. (AK)

*Below* : Teesside provides a plethora of interesting industrial backdrops for the railway photographer as we can see here with BOC towers dominating the view.

The first locomotive in the fleet, 66501, joins the main line at Shell Junction, Lackenby, shortly after leaving Wilton freightliner terminal with 4D89, Wilton - Doncaster freightliner. (PJR)

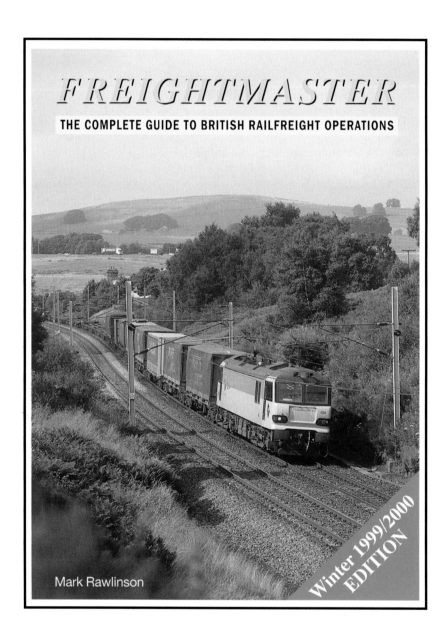

# FREIGHTMASTER

**THE COMPLETE GUIDE TO BRITISH RAILFREIGHT OPERATIONS**

Mark Rawlinson

Winter 1999/2000 EDITION

# FREIGHTMASTER

## THE COMPLETE GUIDE TO BRITISH RAILFREIGHT OPERATIONS

*NEW* WILLESDEN JUNCTION timetable

MILLENNIUM RELAUNCH SPRING 2000

Mark Rawlinson

## MARCH : Intermodal

**(1) :** Freight traffic continues to expand at Ditton with the introduction of a new EWS intermodal service linking Merseyside and East Anglia:

4M08, Harwich   - Ditton

4L84, Ditton    - Harwich

**(2) :** Safeway start using rail to transport goods to the far North of Scotland in containers via the Mossend - Inverness 'Enterprise'; containers for Wick / Thurso are 'tripped' to Georgemas Junction accordingly. Ultimately, a dedicated intermodal service is established between Mossend and Georgemas Junction. The initial services are:

4H44, Mossend   - Inverness

4D66, Inverness   - Mossend

4H45, Inverness   - Georgemas Junction

4H46, Georgemas - Inverness

**(3) :** Start of a new container service from Avonmouth to Tyne Dock conveying Nissan car parts using distinctive green coloured "Seawheel" containers with *Seawheel* branding:

4E41, Avonmouth - Tyne Dock

4V95, Tyne Dock - Avonmouth

*Right* : On this particular occasion, the 'Safeway' train runs as 4H44, the 01:50 Mossend - Georgemas Junction, seen on arrival at Georgemas Junction with 66095 bringing two containers to the terminal. A mechanical crane is used to load / unload containers. Note the VGA wagons stabled in the yard. (AK)

*Above* : The Avonmouth Docks complex dominates the background with the Bulk Import Terminal silo punctuating the skyline on the left. Passing Hallen Marsh Junction, 66161 sets off on the lengthy journey to Tyneside with 4E41, Avonmouth - Tyne Dock intermodal, formed of 14 loaded containers and 6 empty. (AK)

**MARCH** (cont.)

### Locomotives

**(1) :** EWS transfer their fleet of six class 59/2 locomotives to Hither Green. They will work stone trains in London & the South East, releasing class 60's for 'heavier' duties elsewhere.

**(2) :** Having started working 'Enterprise' services between Crewe and Mossend last Summer, the class 92s are now working Anglo-Scottish MGR coal trains between Carlisle and Bescot.

*Above* : The backdrop of Battersea power station is the notable London landmark in view, as 59205 *L. Keith McNair* approaches Wandsworth Road station with 7O96, Acton Yard - Sevington loaded bogie hoppers. (JR)

*Right* : Sweeping round the curve at Heamies Farm, near Norton Bridge, 92024 *Jane Austen* heads 6G04, Carlisle London Road - Bescot, running on this day in the path of 6M40, Ayr - Bescot.

At the time, several of the MGR coal services from Ayr to the West Midlands were hauled by 2 x 37's between Ayr and Carlisle, handing over to a class 92 locomotive for the remainder of the journey. (MB)

### APRIL

### Metals

This month sees a massive blow to freight activity in the Potteries with the closure of the steel works at Etruria, Stoke-on-Trent. This represents the first steel closure since Ravenscraig and an ominous development as steel making will also cease at Llanwern in 2001!

## MARCH / MAY : Mail

The first locomotives of a new 30-strong fleet of class 67 locomotives, specifically built for Royal Mail traffic, start revenue earning service, and will gradually takeover class 47/7s on mail trains. After a slight hiccup on February 29th., when problems prevent 67004 hauling the Swansea - Willesden TPO, the first revenue earning run takes place on March 1st. when 67001 powers the 2320 Willesden - Swansea TPO from Bristol Temple Meads.

To complete the picture, the final Royal Mail Railnet terminal opens at Bristol Parkway on May 15th. and with it a new network (see map *opposite)* of mail train services .The first timetabled service to leave the new terminal is 1S81, the 16:05 service to Shieldmuir hauled, rather surprisingly, by an old class 47 locomotive! This marks the end of mail operations at one of the busiest mail handling stations, Bristol Temple Meads.

*Top* : This is the layout of Bristol Parkway mail terminal as an unidentified class 67 waits to depart with 1S81, the 16:05 Bristol Parkway - Shieldmuir and 37259 waits in the 'up' goods loop.

One can also see the extent of capital investment in 'mail by rail' with terminals and new class 67s and it is rather shameful that all this would finish in less than four years time. (MB)

*Right* : The original class 67 member (67001) is seen in ex-works condition hauling two class 325 units at Plawsworth heading 1M78, the 14:43 Low Fell - Willesden mail; the service being diesel hauled on this occasion due to the derailment of a freight train (6L80, Deanside - Wisbech) at Hambleton, necessitating a diversion off the electrified route. (PJR)

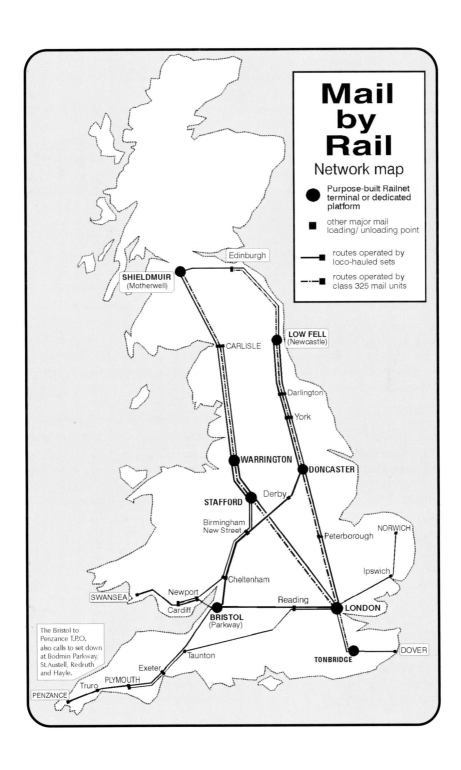

## Mail by Rail
### Network map

● Purpose-built Railnet terminal or dedicated platform

■ other major mail loading/ unloading point

■— routes operated by loco-hauled sets

■-·- routes operated by class 325 mail units

Edinburgh

**SHIELDMUIR** (Motherwell)

CARLISLE

**LOW FELL** (Newcastle)

Darlington

York

**WARRINGTON**

**DONCASTER**

Derby

**STAFFORD**

Birmingham New Street

Peterborough

NORWICH

Ipswich

Cheltenham

Newport

SWANSEA

Cardiff

Reading

**LONDON**

**BRISTOL** (Parkway)

The Bristol to Penzance T.P.O. also calls to set down at Bodmin Parkway, St.Austell, Redruth and Hayle.

Taunton

DOVER

**TONBRIDGE**

Exeter

PLYMOUTH

Truro

PENZANCE

## MAY : Locomotives

MendipRail, responsible for locomotives, wagons and logistical control of rail-borne stone sourced from the Mendip quarries, adopt a new corporate image and 59002 is the first locomotive to bear the new green with orange band livery. Some JNA bogie box wagons have also been repainted in grey livery with 'MRL' branding.

*Right* : Sporting the new livery, *59002 Alan J Day* approaches Westbury with empty box wagons forming 7V67, Sevington - Westbury Yard. (MB)

## Freightliner

Following the installation of heavy lifting cranes at Ditton, container services now run directly to Ditton instead of being 'tripped' from Garston. The first train service is 4F45 from Crewe Basford Hall and further 'direct' services will be introduced in 2001 and 2002, respectively:

| | |
|---|---|
| 4M73, Ipswich Yard - Ditton | 4L71, Ditton - Ipswich Yard |
| 4M45, Ipswich Yard - Ditton | 4L92, Ditton - Ipswich Yard |

In fact, 4M45 / 4L92 are interesting because they come about due to increased business by shipping line Maersk Sealand, enabling them to raise their contracted rail commitment between Felixstowe and Widnes. This also results in Maersk Sealand becoming the first ever shipping line to achieve a record 100,000 containers moving annually by rail through the Port of Felixstowe.

*Above* : From a locomotive perspective, 4M45 / 4L91 are frequently worked by the unique 86501, the sole class 86/5 electric locomotive, so aiding train identification! A lightly loaded 4L92, headed by 86501(re-geared 86608), passes through Rugeley Trent Valley station, which includes in the consist two KQA 'pocket' wagons (introduced in 1998) for carrying 9ft. 6ins. 'high cube' containers.

The 'pocket' wagon is so named because the container sits in a pocket (well) slung between the bogies rather than on top of the wagon, as is the case of a conventional freightliner wagon . (MB)

**MAY** (cont.)

## Construction Materials

Freightliner branch out from their freightliner operations and launch their 'Heavy Haul' division, with the aim of securing other rail-borne freight flows. The first service secured is an existing EWS flow of cement from Earles Sidings to Dewsbury (details below) and, as we shall see later, Freightliner will move into many other freight sectors!

6E79, Earles Sidings - Dewsbury (L)        6M68, Dewsbury - Earles (E)

*Above* : In the cutting on the approach to Oakenshaw Junction, Wakefield, 66503 heads the empty cement tanks (recoded 6M89 when this photograph was taken) bound for Earles Sidings in the Hope Valley. The City of Wakefield skyline provides the backdrop. (MR)

## JUNE

### Metals

A new steel terminal opens at Seaforth, Liverpool, and with it a new freight service:

6M09, Lackenby - Seaforth (L)          6E82, Seaforth - Lackenby (E)

### Automotive

Freightliner take over the transportation of imported Ford vehicles through Southampton Western Docks from EWS with an amended service:

6M16, Southampton  - Crewe B. H. (L)

6046, Crewe B. H.   - Southampton (E)

*Right* : Heading north along the main line between Oxford and Banbury, 47197 passes the popular photogenic location of Kings Sutton with 6M16, Southampton Western Docks - Crewe Basford Hall Yard with a lengthy rake of imported Ford vans and cars. The church at Kings Sutton dominates the skyline. (JR)

### Construction Materials

Freightliner Heavy Haul secure another new cement service, this time linking the cement works at Hope with Blue Circle's new distribution plant at Weaste, Manchester. The new terminal officially opens on July 28th. and is situated on the long disused rail-served quay on the Manchester Ship Canal:

6J91, Earles Sidings - Weaste (L)          6H92, Weaste - Earles (E)

*Above* : Some Canada Geese take time out from the waters of the Manchester Ship Canal adjacent to the new cement terminal, where 66503 has just arrived with a rake of loaded cement tanks from Earles Sidings. (PS)

# FREIGHTMASTER

## THE COMPLETE GUIDE TO BRITISH RAILFREIGHT OPERATIONS

**NEW** Royal Mail Schedules

Summer & Autumn 2000

Mark Rawlinson

### JULY

## Minerals

English China Clay introduce new JIA china clay tanks in distinctive blue livery with Imerys branding. These wagons will replace polybulk wagons used for the china clay export traffic on the existing service linking Exeter Riverside and Dollands Moor, viz; 6O92 (L) / 6V95 (E).

*Above* : Some of the new JIA wagons can be seen behind 66236 as it waits to leave Exeter Riverside yard with 6O92, (Mondays only) Exeter Riverside - Dollands Moor. (DM)

## Coal

EWS secure a new 10 year contract to move coal to Fifoots (Uskmouth) power station, but commissioning problems delay the opening of the power station and although the flow of coal starts running later, it will be rather intermittent to say the least - ending completely within two years following the closure of the power station. The coal being sourced through Newport Docks, plus Avonmouth and Parc Slip.

Power stations with flue gas desulphurisation require Lime and the planning consent for Fifoots means the use of rail to get it there. The Lime originates from Peak Forest and is 'tripped' from Newport ADJ in CSA wagons.

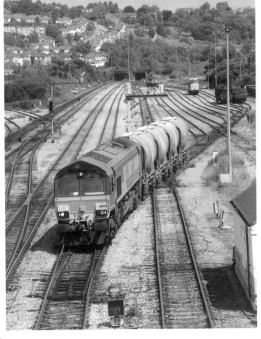

*Right:* : 66036 propels 4 empty CSA Lime tanks into a rather deserted Alexandra Dock Junction Yard, forming 6F06 ex-Fifoots; 56025 and 37308 are also visible (MB)

*Opposite Page* : Having been given the road, 66247 leaves East Usk Yard, Newport, for the 3-mile trip to Uskmouth with 6F24, the 09:45 Avonmouth - Fifoots. (MB)

### AUGUST : 'Enterprise'

This month marks the end of the line for the well known 'petfood' service, formed of VGA wagons, which ran initially via the WCML over Beattock and Shap until being re-routed via the ECML:

6L80,  Deanside - Wisbech (L)                    6S93,  Wisbech - Deanside (E)

*Above* : In happier times, Loadhaul-liveried 56084 sweeps past Greskine with 6L80, Deanside - Wisbech. (PJR)

### SEPTEMBER : Metals

A rail loading facility at Skinningrove on the Boulby branch is commissioned for Corus. Although there is a daily Lackenby to Skinningrove service, which brings in steel blooms, finished products have not left the plant by rail for many years.

*Above :* Skinningrove produces specialised steel products for export, especially for use in the shipbuilding industry. Outside the steel plant, 66068 waits to leave with a special train of finished steel for Tees Yard. (AK)

**SEPTEMBER** (cont.)

## Coal

A new coal loading facility opens at New Cumnock, on the former GSWR route. The site stems from a Government grant of £2.5 million awarded to Hamilton-based firm L.A.W. Mining Ltd and will see 1.6 million tonnes of coal moved by rail - equivalent to some 170,000 lorries.

*Right* : Looking across the running lines of the ex-GSW Route at New Cumnock, 66544 waits at the loading point, while HHAs are loaded with coal before leaving with 6Z42, the 12:15 service to Eggborough power station. Note, this photograph was taken after the HHAs were introduced in 2001! (IL)

## Freightliner

A new freightliner / intermodal site opens at Grangemouth on behalf of TDG Nexus and marks the beginning of a significant increase in traffic to Grangemouth. The first service is operated by Freightliner (running as a special, coded 4Z50) bringing containers from Coatbridge to Grangemouth, with the locomotive returning light engine to Mossend.

Ultimately, 4Z50 will later be replaced by a new EWS service from Trafford Park to Grangemouth.

*Above* : This new service brings the colourful sight of a container train to central Scotland during daylight hours, as we see here with 47150 passing Greenhill Lower Junction with 4Z50, Coatbridge - Grangemouth. (IL)

## OCTOBER : Minerals

A new flow of containerised Lime starts operating from Thrislington to Margam using 'Rail Freight Services' containers for use in the blast furnaces at Port Talbot steelworks. The details are:

6V02, Thrislington - Margam (L)

6E86, Margam - Thrislington (E)

*Right* : A subsequent ammendment to the service sees the Lime 'tripped' from Thrislington, going forward with empty steel wagons as 6V02, Tees Yard - Margam. On a cold and frosty Winter morning, 56071 passes Stillington on the Tursdale Junction - Norton Junction(s) freight line with 6N91, Thrislington - Tees Yard 'trip'. (PJR)

## Express Parcels

Tasker Street (Walsall) Express Freight Terminal becomes operational for the purpose of moving parcels quickly and efficiently around the country. Unfortunately, the Hatfield rail accident results in the service being suspended because speed restrictions hinder the benefits on offer. Fortunately, the service does eventually get off the ground, with Securicor the first customer.

The service operates as:

1S03, Walsall - Aberdeen

5D03, Aberdeen - Motherwell,
1M03, Motherwell - Walsall

A year later sees an additional service start up between Law Junction and Inverness.

*Above* : Amidst wonderful scenery, 67025 *Western Star* heads 5D03, Aberdeen - Motherwell empty vans, at Bardrill Road. This location is between Gleneagles and Blackford and is the 'dividing line' between the Gleneagles Estates and the Blackford Estates. (IL)

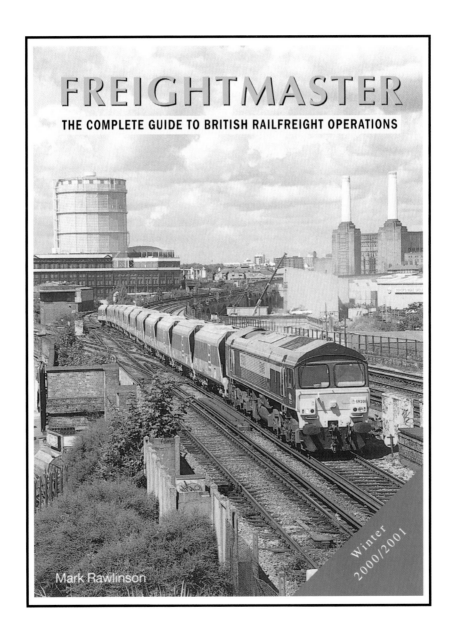

# FREIGHTMASTER

## THE COMPLETE GUIDE TO BRITISH RAILFREIGHT OPERATIONS

Winter 2000/2001

Mark Rawlinson

## NOVEMBER

### Coal - Rolling Stock

Within days of each other, both Freightliner and EWS show off their new coal wagons. This is an especially important step for Freightliner's Heavy Haul division as they set out to secure a big chunk of the coal market from EWS!

**(1)** : Freightliner's new coal hoppers are coded HHA and are built by Wagony Swidnica, Poland, each with a carrying capacity of 73.6 tonnes and a top speed of 75mph. These new wagons will be ostensibly used for imported and Anglo-Scottish coal traffic.

**(2)** : EWS start taking delivery of their new HTA coal wagons for use on MGR circuits around the UK, painted in EWS red livery, and are the first of a £50m order for 845 state-of-the-art wagons. Part of EWS' fleet modernisation, this order is the largest for one specific type of railway wagon since 1976 and each wagon is capable of carrying 75 tonnes at a top speed of 75mph.

*Above* : When clean, the new EWS HTA hoppers make a fine sight as evidenced in this photograph of 66243 passing Kingsbury brick works with empty HTA's heading back to Toton from Rugeley power station.

*Opposite Page* : Snaking across the junction to take the Castleford route, 66549 heads 6G03, the 12:15 Immingham - Ferrybridge '*Heavy Haul* ' coal service at Milford Junction. Coal services passing through Milford Junction en-route to Ferrybridge have to take a circuitous route via Castleford, Pontefract Monkhill and Ferrybridge Junction, as access to the power station can only be gained from the south. (MB)

### Locomotives

The two British Steel blue liveried class 60 locomotives (60006 & 60033) are repainted into Corus silver grey livery, the colours of British Steel's successor.

This event coming only 3 months before Corus announce a massive reduction in steel making in South Wales!

*Right* : Not on steel duties, but a fine sight all the same; 60006 *Scunthorpe Ironmaster* on aggregate duties at Peak Forest having worked in with 6H55, the ARC stone empties from Bletchley. (PJR)

### FEBRUARY : Metals

**(1) :** Corus undertake a review of steel making operations and announce they are to cease steel production at Llanwern steelworks in South Wales. The downside is the withdrawal of the Port Talbot - Llanwern iron ore tipplers (the last train running on May 25th.) along with MGR coal trains to the plant. The upside is that the rolling mills remain in use and will result in large quantities of steel slab being moved by rail from Lackenby to Llanwern for rolling.

*Above* : These 'slab' trains run seven days a week and although 'booked' for class 60 operation it is not uncommon for other locomotive classes to put in an appearance. With the River Tees in the background, 66167 approaches Tees Yard in charge of a fully laden 6V43, (Sun) Lackenby - Llanwern. (MB)

*Below* : One of these 'slab' trains (6V37, Lackenby - Llanwern), headed by 60079 *Foinaven,* is seen passing South Bank, an area of heavy industry where extensive track rationalisation has taken place. (AK)

**(2) :** A further consequence will be the end of freight traffic on the Park Junction - Ebbw Vale line because, as part of the Corus review, the tinplate works at Ebbw Vale will also close in due course. To record this happening two photographs of the site are reproduced below:

Before and after .......

*Above* Left : The yard at Ebbw Vale as seen in prosperous times. Wagonloads of rolled steel can be seen in the yard, which will be made into tinplate and despatched by rail. Three Ferrywagons leave the yard behind 37903, forming 6B38, Ebbw Vale - Newport Alexandra Dock Junction yard. (AK)

*Above Right* : The same view after traffic ceased and the commencement of demolition. (AK)

**(3) :** However, there is still a requirement for tinplate and ECCS (Chromium plated steel) which will continue to be produced at the Corus Trostre works near Llanelli; the material for which is hot rolled coil supplied from Port Talbot steelworks in specially designed wagons.

*Above* : The other Corus grey-liveried locomotive (60033 *Tees Steel Express*) is seen passing Waungron on the Swansea District Line hauling hot rolled coil forming 6B48, Margam - Trostre. (AK)

## FEBRUARY (cont.) : Freightliner

On 13 February 2001, the last freightliner leaves Pengam freightliner terminal, Cardiff, with 47289 hauling 4L56, the 20:05 Cardiff Pengam - Felixstowe.

However, a brand new terminal opens at Wentloog, four miles east of Cardiff, known as SWIFT (South Wales International Freight Terminal) occupying 25 acres and is twice the size of the old Pengam terminal.

66503 and 47323 work the two trains scheduled to leave on the opening day: 4S81 to Coatbridge and 4L56 to Felixstowe, respectively.

*Right* : The official opening does not take place until 23 March 2001 when 66506 *Crewe Regeneration* officiates by breaking the banner at the opening ceremony . (AK)

## Intermodal

DRS extend their operating base by linking up with W H Malcolm to provide traction for a new intermodal service between Daventry and Grangemouth involving 2 x DRS 37's hauling a rake of former Rover 'Cube' wagons. The first run takes place on Valentines Day conveying glass jars from Alloa for use with Nescafe:

4M30, Grangemouth - Daventry          4S49, Daventry - Grangemouth

*Above* : With two wagons sporting the house colours of W H Malcolm, 37612 + 37609 depart from Grangemouth with 4M30 and will work the train throughout via Mossend and the WCML, returning to Scotland on 4S49. (IL)

# FREIGHTMASTER

## THE NATIONAL RAILFREIGHT TIMETABLE

**NOW** Quarterly

No. 21
March to June
2001

Mark Rawlinson

## MARCH

### New Freight Operator - Great Britain Rail Freight

New operator Great Britain Rail Freight (GBRf), a subsidiary of GB Railway, enters the railfreight market with 7 new class 66/7 locomotives (67001 - 66707) painted in a striking 'bluebird' livery and based at Willesden. They have a 92,000 lbf tractive effort and a maximum speed of 75mph.

*Above* : The initial business will be to power trains serving infrastructure sites in the east of England and East Anglia supporting Railtrack renewal and maintenance projects. One of the new locomotives, 66706, approaches Mill Hill Broadway station with Railtrack self-discharge hoppers forming 6L19, the 12:20 Wellingborough - Temple Mills. (NG)

### APRIL : Automotive

The former Ford plant at Halewood, Merseyside, is reborn, but this time manufacturing 'top of the range' Jaguar cars.

*Right* : Jaguar invests heavily in new railfreight facilities at its Halewood plant (also Castle Bromwich in January 2003) enabling the Company to distribute some of its export business by rail.

At Halewood, 66092 leaves the loading area on 23rd. April with the first train of Jaguar cars, conveyed in enclosed WIA wagons to protect the valuable merchandise!. (PS)

### JUNE : Intermodal / 'Enterprise'

**(1)** : On behalf of 'DIY' retailer B. & Q., EWS start a new service from Warrington to Deanside. The train (4Z59) runs direct to Deanside on the outward journey with the containers returning on 4M38, Deanside - Daventry as far as Arpley Yard, where they are then 'tripped' to Dallam.

**(2)** : Having lost the Vinyl Chloride Monomer traffic to coastal shipping two years ago, Dow Corning and BP traffic increases to daily with a new container service between Newport Alexandra Dock Junction and Barry Docks.

*Above* : Dallam freight terminal is situated on the 'up' side of the WCML where we see a container being loaded in readiness for 56110 to leave with 4Z59, the 11:29 Dallam - Deanside 'Dreambox'. (PS)

*Below* : At Barry Docks, 09003 shunts wagons from the morning's 6B06 'Enterprise' service from Newport ADJ. (AK)

**JUNE** (cont.)

### 'Enterprise'

A new flow starts this month (similar to 6L71, Immingham - Ripple Lane) transporting newsprint conveyed in Ferrywagons.

The service is from Immingham to Knowsley, Greater Manchester, which runs in both directions via Diggle and proves to be a 'solid' class 56 turn right up to the withdrawal of the class in March 2004:

  6M30,  Immingham - Knowsley (L)

  6E30,  Knowsley    - Immingham (E)

Following on from this, a similar service starts operating involving the importation of paper through the Port of Felixstowe using cargowaggons. This flow is :

  6E57,  Felixstowe   - Healey Mills (L)

  6L56,  Healey Mills - Felixstowe (E)

*Top Right* : The returning empty ferrywagons bound for Immingham (6E30) are seen at Belle Vue, Wakefield, having passed Calder Bridge Junction hauled by 'Dutch' liveried 56049. At the rear of the train are three other wagons, which are returning to Immingham, having been attached at Healey Mills. (MB)

*Right* : This is the originating point for 6E57, the new Felixstowe Creek paper sidings, where Barclay 0-6-0 shunter No. 01 531 can be seen stabled. (IS)

*Below* : Ex-BR shunting locomotives also see use at the Potter Group terminal at Knowsley and two are seen shunting a single Ferrywagon, 08598 and 08202, both sporting a rather garish yellow livery! (IS)

# FREIGHTMASTER

## THE NATIONAL RAILFREIGHT TIMETABLE

Mark Rawlinson

No. 22

July to September 2001

## JULY : Metals

After a gap of 18 months, steel traffic returns to Brierley Hill in the West Midlands with a trainload of billet / bars:

6M26, Scunthorpe - Brierley Hill (L)    6E87, Brierley Hill - Scunthorpe (E)

### Construction Materials

Freightliner continue to expand their operations by moving into the construction materials sector, initially moving ballast to the LDC at Crewe Basford Hall, sourced from quarries at Penmaenmawr, Shap and Stud Farm.

*Right* : The sidings at Penmaenmawr Quarry are situated adjacent to the main A55 trunk road and, with loading complete, 66606 waits to leave with 6K22, Penmaenmawr - Crewe Basford Hall ballast. (RN)

### Automotive

Imported Ford vehicles from Creutzwald arrive at Corby via the Channel Tunnel and a new service (6X75) sees onward transportation to Washwood Heath.

*Right* : Transrail-liveried 56049 leaves Corby Hub with 6X75, Corby - Washwood Heath.

Usually, this train takes the direct route via Nuneaton but, when it runs 'out of gauge' it will travel via Stenson Junction, thus avoiding Arley Tunnel on the Nuneaton to Water Orton line. (JR)

### AUGUST : Express Parcels

EWS launch a second express courier parcels service, this time between Motherwell and Inverness. The train continues to use specially adapted vans, which return from Inverness in the consist of 4D65, Inverness-Mossend 'Enterprise.

*Right* : In the Pass of Druimuachdar, at Crubenmore, 67030 is seen in charge of 1Z30, the 05:40 Law Junction - Inverness Securicor parcels. The A9 Perth - Inverness trunk road is in the background. (PJR)

## SEPTEMBER : Petroleum

**(1)** : More business for Freightliner as they secure a contract form Conoco to operate oil trains between Humber Refinery and Kingsbury. The respective service is detailed below and is enhanced in appearance by the introduction of a new rake of blue livery bogie tanks:

6M08,  Humber - Kingsbury (L)                6E55,  Kingsbury - Humber (E)

**(2)** : After 10 years absence, oil traffic returns to Lairg. The oil tanks are conveyed on  EWS 'Enterprise' services; 6H45, Mossend - Inverness extended to Lairg on Tuesday, the empties returning on 6D46, Inverness - Mossend, starting back from Lairg on Thursdays.

*Above* : Having left the Birmingham - Derby main line at Stenson Junction, 66604 heads 6E55, formed of new  blue TEA tank wagons, at Findern on the 'freight only' line to Sheet Stores Junction. (JR)

*Below* :  At the destination, 37411 *The Scottish Railway Preservation Society* reverses into the terminal at Lairg having arrived with the fuel oil tanks on 6H61, (TO) Inverness - Lairg, 'Enterprise' trip. (AK)

# FREIGHTMASTER

## THE NATIONAL RAILFREIGHT TIMETABLE

Mark Rawlinson

No. 23
October to December
2001

## NOVEMBER

### Channel Tunnel Freight

Channel traffic is thrown into chaos by SNCF suspending all freight services due to security problems with the nightly invasion of UK-bound (would be) asylum seekers at Frethun.

By the end of the month, some 'Chunnel' traffic resumes but, due to enhanced security, including double-manning of all trains between Frethun and Dollands Moor, throughput reduces by some 50%.

*Right* : A typical scene at Frethun Yard with two class 92 locomotives to the fore: 92012 *Thomas Hardy* + 92010 *Moliere*. (PS)

## DECEMBER

### Domestic Waste

Having moved into the domestic waste market earlier in the year by taking over the Avon 'Binliner', Freightliner continue to secure new business from EWS, this time the movement of domestic waste between Cricklewood and Forders Sidings.

*Above* : The landfill site at Forders Sidings lies on the Bedford St. Johns to Fenny Stratford line and 66553 leaves Forders Sidings (suitably adorned with headboard) with 6C51, Forders - Cricklewood empty refuse containers. (NG)

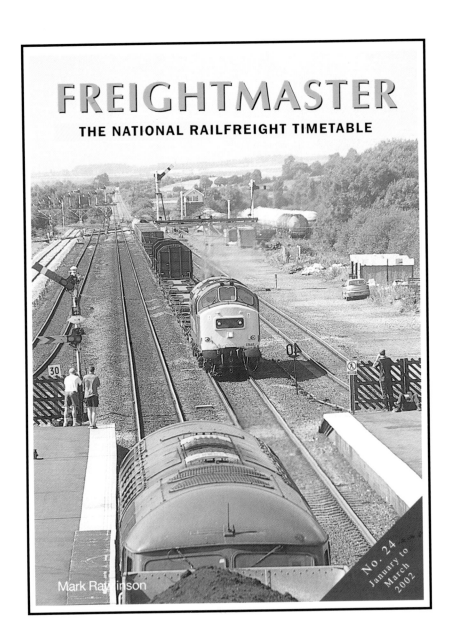

# FREIGHTMASTER

## THE NATIONAL RAILFREIGHT TIMETABLE

Mark Rawlinson

No. 24
January to
March
2002

## JANUARY

### Petroleum

Murco and Petroplus introduce a splash of colour on the petroleum flows which serve their terminals at Bedworth, Theale and Westerleigh with the introduction of new red TEA bogie tank wagons.

The terminals receive petroleum from Robeston refinery at Milford Haven and Port Clarence, Teeside.

*Right* : Several of the red bogie tanks can be seen behind 60054 *Charles Babbage* as it makes its way along the 'down' goods line at Pilning with 6B33, Theale - Robeston petroleum empties. (MB)

### Freight Operations

Some seven miles of single track reopens on the Portishead branch (Nr. Bristol) to serve Portbury Docks, with initial freight services of imported coal to Fifoots, Ironbridge and Rugeley power stations.

*Below* : This is a section of the new Portbury branch, close to the River Avon. On an embankment which carries the railway line under the M5 road bridge at Avonmouth, 66068 heads back to Portbury with 6V23, the 07:02 MGR empties from Washwood Heath. (IS)

## FEBRUARY

### Intermodal

GBRf expand their operations with a new contract from Medite Shipping to convey containers from Felixstowe to Doncaster/Selby (thrice weekly) and Hams Hall (twice weekly):

6E78, Felixstowe - Selby

6M73, Felixstowe - Hams Hall

6L79, Selby     - Felixstowe

6L72, Hams Hall - Felixstowe

*Above* : A classic photographic location.... the magnificent sight of of Ely cathedral dominates the view as 66711 heads further out of East Anglia with the twice weekly intermodal service  (6M73) from Felixstowe to Hams Hall. (JR)

## MARCH

### Mail

The Royal Mail, in an attempt to reduce losses, announce cutbacks in its rail distribution by withdrawing some services:

1V04, 16:35 Shieldmuir - Bristol Parkway

1S00, 00:10 London     - Shieldmuir

1V37, 22:48 Swansea   - London

Further services will be withdrawn on a gradual basis until the Royal Mail's contract with EWS expires in March 2004; mail trains first started running on the railways way back in 1830!.

### Minerals

New rolling stock appears on the Boulby branch; NACCO-owned JIA hoppers, hired to Cleveland Potash, for use on the Boulby potash / rock salt traffic.

*Opposite Page* : A natural haven in an otherwise heavy industrial area.... 56071 passes Coatham Marsh nature reserve, Redcar, with 6F75, Tees Dock - Boulby potash empties, which include some JIA hoppers already showing the signs of extensive use on the Boulby circuit. These wagons are also used to convey rock salt from the Boulby mine. (MB)

# FREIGHTMASTER

## THE NATIONAL RAILFREIGHT TIMETABLE

Mark Rawlinson

No. 25
April to June
2002

## MAY : Infrastructure

As construction of the CTRL gathers pace, a purpose built site for the holding of locomotives, wagons and materials is constructed at Beechbrook Farm (near Ashford) which, after completion of this stage of the CTRL, will be made good and returned to its natural habitat of fields.

Preserved locomotive, D8142 (*Above Left*) , is working on the CTRL at Beechbrook at the head of a wire train, while four Freightliner class 66/5 locomotives Nos. 66554 / 530 / 529 / 610 (*Above Right*) are stabled in the yard and await their next turns of duty. (Both IS)

## Chemicals

Apart from nuclear traffic, the most dangerous freight flow on the railway system is the movement of Hydrocyanic Acid between Seals Sands and Haverton Hill. This flow ceases this month with the deadly chemical being piped instead. This 'trip' always ran as a class 8 special:

8X03, Seal Sands - Haverton Hill (L)      8X04, Haverton Hill - Seal Sands (E)

*Above* : On the north bank of the River Tees, at Port Clarence, 56113 returns to Seal Sands with 8X04, HCN empties. Note the safety factor, the inclusion of two 'barrier' wagons between the locomotive and the first tank wagon. This view also provides a close up of the famous Middlesbrough transporter bridge. (PJR)

### JUNE : Automotive

Portbury Docks continues to see increased freight traffic with a new flow commencing this month with the transportation of imported cars to Mossend operated by Freightliner. The initial service is weekly but soon increases to a thrice weekly service:

6S41, Portbury - Mossend (L)  6V14, Mossend - Portbury (E)

An illustration of this service can be found on Page 141.

### Construction Materials

A new freight terminal opens at Seaham, near Sunderland, on the site of the old Dawdon Colliery to handle cement, general merchandise and steel. However, it is only cement traffic which materialises with two dedicated flows, operated by Freightliner:

6E26, Earles   - Seaham (L)
6M27, Seaham  - Earles (E)

6E90, Oxwellmains - Seaham (L)
6S96, Seaham - Oxwellmains (E)

*Right* : A general view; a deserted Seaham freight handling facility along with the cement terminal in the background. (IS)

### Freightliner

New services introduced onto the freightliner network:

4V50, Southampton - Cardiff  4O51, Cardiff - Southampton
4L86, Thamesport  - Tilbury  4O87, Tilbury - Thamesport

*Above* : Most traffic between South Wales and the South Coast goes via Westbury. However, a pleasing addition to the timetable is a new daytime freightliner service via Swindon, routed this way in order to preserve route knowledge for Freightliner train crews. Passing a very overgrown siding at Highworth Junction, Swindon, 57010 *Freightliner Crusader* heads east in charge of 4O51, Cardiff Wentloog - Southampton Millbrook freightliner. (MB)

# FREIGHTMASTER

## THE NATIONAL RAILFREIGHT TIMETABLE

Mark Rawlinson

No. 26
July to
September
2002

## JULY

### Intermodal

**(1) :** GBRf expand their operation with Medite Shipping Company with the Felixstowe to Hams Hall and Selby services going over to daily running; 66709 is painted in Medite black livery to commemorate the occasion and named *Joseph Arnold Davies* after the father of Medite's Managing Director, Roy Davies.

**(2) :** EWS secure a new intermodal service which replaces 4Z50, Coatbridge - Grangemouth freightliner, running as 4S67, Trafford Park - Grangemouth and 4M67 return.

*Above* : The celebrity 66709 passes Stenson Junction with 4M21, Felixstowe - Hams Hall intermodal. (RN)

*Below* : Since its opening in September 2000, heavy lifting gear has been installed at the TDG Nexus terminal, Grangemouth, as seen here with 66096 waiting to depart with 4M67 to Trafford Park. (PS)

## JULY (cont.)

### Metals

Bad news...the closure of the Allied Steel & Wire (ASW) plant at Tremorfa, Cardiff, resulting in a complete revamp of scrap metal services with several being withdrawn altogether.

*Right* : One casualty of the ASW closure is the loss of 6V99, (FO) Hamworthy - Cardiff Tidal scrap train, which also collects scrap from Swindon en-route to Cardiff. With two cooling towers at Didcot power station dominating the background, 6V99 passes Milton on the 'down' goods line with 60022 hauling the train. (MB)

## SEPTEMBER

### Metals

A new steel service is introduced following the re-opening of the the line to Chatham Docks:

    6U84,  Chatham Docks - Hoo Junction (L)

    6U83,  Hoo Junction - Chatham Docks (E)

### Intermodal

EWS introduce some new services to complement the Intermodal network, including:

| | | | | | |
|---|---|---|---|---|---|
| 6Z14, | Southampton W. D. - Wakefield | | 6Z90, | Wakefield - Southampton W. D. | |
| 4M10, | Southampton W. D. - Ditton | | 4O05, | Ditton | - Southampton W. D. |
| 4M43, | Felixstowe | - Ditton | 4L72, | Ditton | - Felixstowe |

*Above* : Passing Banbury North, 66230 heads a well loaded 4Z10, the 05:18 Southampton Western Docks - Ditton, photographed at a time when the train ran as a special (Z), prior to being recoded as 4M10. (NG)

## SEPTEMBER (cont.)

### Freight Operations

The re-opening of closed lines and the return of freight traffic is always pleasing to report as is this case study in the Midlands. Work started in 2001 to construct a rail link from Kingsbury to a new rail-served distribution facility at Birch Coppice, North Warwickshire. The line courses the site of the former mineral branch to both Birch Coppice and Baddesley coal sites.

A considerable amount of engineering work was undertaken to complete the new rail link and two photographs are included to illustrate this.

The sole freight service over the re-opened line is a daily 'Enterprise' trip to Birch Coppice bringing in automotive components for Volkswagen from Germany via the Channel Tunnel:

6G36, Bescot        - Birch Coppice (L)

6G42, Birch Coppice - Bescot (E)

*Top Right* : Near Baddesley, the new line was laid more than 10ft. lower than the original level to facilitate a road bridge to a new business park, which 66230 has passed under on its way to work the 6G42 'trip' to Bescot. (MB)

*Right* : Looking in the opposite direction, work was still being carried out in 2004 to strengthen embankments, which have been completely denuded of trees, much to the displeasure of local residents! (MB)

*Below* : As the morning sunshine struggles to break through, 37503 heads 6G36, Bescot - Birch Coppice 'Enterprise' over the River Tame at Lea Marston. (MB)

**SEPTEMBER** (cont.)

### Locomotives

The remaining class 58 locomotives are withdrawn, even though a good number are in excellent working order; a legacy of too many class 66's!

The class started life on MGR coal trains in the Midlands but ended up working aggregate, departmental and 'Enterprise' trains in the South of England.

*Right* : 58045 passes through Moreton cutting with 7V27, Eastleigh - Didcot Yard departmental. (MB)

### 'Enterprise'

Any new flow of freight traffic on the Great Western Mainline between Bristol and London is always welcome and this month sees an addition to the 'Enterprise' network with a daily service bringing paper to Avonmouth:

6V53, Wembley - Avonmouth (L)          6M33, Avonmouth - Wembley (E)

*Above* : Passing Didcot East, 66218 proceeds along the 'up' main line in charge of 6M33, Avonmouth - Wembley 'Enterprise'. This working is a solid '66' turn although two years later it is not uncommon for 6M33 to be hauled by a pair of class 67 locomotives, since becoming available for work following the withdrawal of mail trains from the network. (MB)

# FREIGHTMASTER

## THE NATIONAL RAILFREIGHT TIMETABLE

Mark Rawlinson

No. 27
October to
December
2002

# FREIGHTMASTER

## THE NATIONAL RAILFREIGHT TIMETABLE

Mark Rawlinson

No. 28
January to
March
2003

## FEBRUARY : Coal

Freightliner *Heavy Haul* reach a significant milestone having operated its 10,000th coal train. The Company now handles about 25% of trains in the coal sector using a fleet of 19 sets of 17 stainless steel HHA wagons - a considerable achievement in just over two years!

## Construction Materials

A trainload of flyash is now running between West Burton power station to Selby using MBA 'Monster' box wagons, which were originally ordered by EWS back in 1998 and delivered the following year. The new flow is:

6D90,  West Burton - Selby (L)          6D86,  Selby - West Burton (E)

*Opposite Page* : The use of a telephoto lens helps to foreshorten this view of 66020 passing Milford Junction with a rake of empty MBA box wagons en-route with 6D86, Selby - West Burton power station. (MB)

## MARCH : Automotive

Jaguar cars open a railhead at Castle Bromwich, Birmingham, to export new cars and to mark the occasion, 60065 is named *Spirit of Jaguar*. The cars for the export market have a dedicated service and are moved to Southampton Eastern Docks in covered car carriers to avoid damage and vandalism:

4O20,  Washwood Heath - Southampton (L)   4M49,  Southampton - Castle Bromwich (E)

## Metals

Following the closure of Allied Steel & Wire and the loss of associated scrap services, it is pleasing to report that EWS are introducing new services to move scrap metal from Tavistock Junction (Plymouth), Hamworthy and Swindon to South Wales:

6Z25,  Hamworthy    - Newport Docks (L)   6Z15,  Newport - Hamworthy (E)

6G68,  Tavistock Jct. - Cardiff Docks (L)   6G67,  Cardiff   - Tavistock Jct. (E)

6G86,  Swindon       - Cardiff Docks (L)   6H65,  Cardiff   - Swindon (E)

It is also interesting to note that Newport Docks is receiving timetabled trains of scrap for the first time ever; previously, scrap trains had run as one off specials.

*Above* : Stabled in Cocklebury Yard, Swindon, a lengthy rake of scrap wagons (6G86 to Cardiff Docks) waits to leave behind 56018 *Stanton,* which will propel the wagons out of the sidings in order to gain access to the main line. (MB)

## MARCH (cont.)

### Coal

Two coal-fired power stations close in the East Midlands; High Marnham, thus condemning a 15-mile remnant of the Lancashire, Derbyshire & East Coast Railway and Drakelow, near Burton-upon-Trent, which was served by a branch off the Leicester - Coalville line.

*Above* : With the power station on the horizon, 66086 departs from High Marnham with the penultimate train on the branch; 6W22, the 14:18 High Marnham - Worksop MGR empties. (CB)

### Minerals

GB Railfreight take over the running of gypsum trains from EWS (illustrated later), starting with:

   4Y81,  Southampton W. D. - Mountfield (L)    4Y19,  Mountfield - Southampton (E)

To inaugurate the new traffic, GBRf run its first train headed by 66704 + 66711 on 6Y19, Mountfield - Southampton, with the leading locomotive carrying a 'GBRf Gypsum' headboard. The train is worked as far as Eastleigh by 66711, where 66704 is put on the front and the pair go forward to the docks.

### Infrastructure

Considerable work has been carried out at the ballast 'tip' at Chaddesden, Derby, to make it a 'Virtual Quarry' for use on the WCML upgrade work in the Stoke-on-Trent area.

### APRIL

### Mail

More mail cutbacks announced - this time the first withdrawal of a TPO:

   1V68,  19:46 Shieldmuir - Cardiff       1S09,  20:05 Cardiff - Shieldmuir

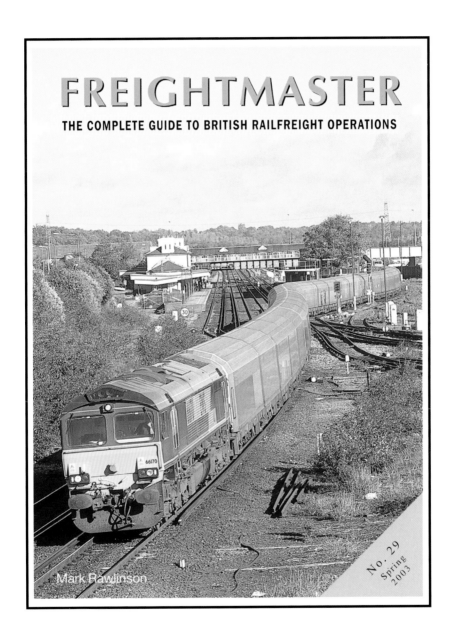

# FREIGHTMASTER

## THE COMPLETE GUIDE TO BRITISH RAILFREIGHT OPERATIONS

Mark Rawlinson

No. 29
Spring
2003

## MAY : Construction Materials

In conjunction with the Heathrow Terminal 5 project, Freightliner operate a new cement flow while EWS also secure a slice of the action by moving pulverised flyash from West Burton power station. The respective services are:

| | | | | |
|---|---|---|---|---|
| 6V27, | Earles | - Colnbrook (L) | 6M84, | Colnbrook - Earles (E) |
| 6V25, | West Burton | - Colnbrook (L) | 6E94, | Colnbrook - West Burton (E) |

*Above* : This is a view of the Colnbrook terminal, which is situated at the end of a 3-mile 'freight only' branch line from West Drayton; 66529 has arrived with 6V27, Earles - Colnbrook cement and there are also some of the distinctive orange coloured ISO flyash tanks on the right-handside of the terminal. (PS)

*Below* : On the return leg, 66559 passes Oakley (north of Bedford) on the Midland mainline with 6M84, Colnbrook - Earles cement empties. (NG)

No apology is made for the overkill, but the distinctive West Burton - Colnbrook flyash train is a most welcome and colourful addition to the railfreight scene!

*Top* : At the start of the journey, 66196 waits to leave West Burton power station with 6V25, loaded ISO tanks bound for Colnbrook. (CB)

*Right* : A view to illustrate a section of the seldom photographed Gainsborough Lea Road to Lincoln line and 66020 hauling 6V25 past Gate Burton, near Stow Park. (CB)

*Below* : The orange ISO tanks make a fine sight as 66220 heads 6V25 along the ECML towards Peterborough, near Tallington. (JR)

## MAY (cont.) Intermodal

In direct competition with Freightliner, EWS sets up a nationwide network of intermodal services. The central 'hub' is Wembley yard and other services connect at Willesden Euroterminal or run direct between terminals.

Branded "Intermodal Express", it comprises a mixture of existing and brand new services. New services include:

| | | |
|---|---|---|
| 4Z55, | Ditton | - Thamesport |
| 4M28, | Thamesport | - Ditton |
| 4Z84, | Grangemouth | - Daventry |
| 4S78, | Daventry | - Grangemouth |
| 4Z14, | Willesden | - Wakefield |
| 4Z90, | Wakefield | - Willesden |
| 6Z90, | Willesden | - Southampton W. D. |
| 6Z74, | Southampton | - Willesden |

Wakefield Freight Centre, situated between Normanton and Castleford, has seen a steady growth in traffic since opening and here we take the opportunity to take a look at the terminal and one of its associated services.

*Top Right* : At Belle Vue, Wakefield, 66150 heads a well loaded 6L55, Wakefield - Felixstowe intermodal, making its way to the ECML at Doncaster via Oakenshaw Junction, Hare Park Junction and South Elmsall. The train has just past Calder Bridge Junction, which is visible at the end of the rake of containers. (MB)

*Below* : 66077 on arrival at Wakefield Freight Centre with 6E98, Wembley - Wakefield 'Enterprise' / intermodal. (PS)

## JUNE

### Construction materials

**(1)** : Freightliner start a completely new service for Lafarge conveying cement from Westbury cement works to Southampton Millbrook, using a fleet of Babcock 'Mega 3' KAA intermodal wagons, which carry road trailers 'piggyback' style.

6O77,  Westbury - Millbrook (L)          6V77,  Millbrook - Westbury (E)

**(2)** : Freightliner also secure a contract to move blast furnace slag from Teesside to Cambridgeshire using the under-utilised 'Bow-Waste' containers. The use of the 'Bow waste' wagons are a temporary measure before Freightliner's new box wagons are delivered, which will also see use on aggregate flows around the country:

6L01,  Port Clarence - Chesterton Jct. (L)      6D38,  Chesterton Jct. - Port Clarence (E)

*Top* : This is the scene at Millbrook freightliner terminal, Southampton, where 47270 *Corby Brothers 1842-1992* is about to leave with a trainload of empty cement lorries forming 6V77, Millbrook - Westbury.

A solitary Blue Circle road trailer remains in Millbrook yard, which shows the type of trailer being used in this unique operation. (MB)

*Right* : The blue coloured 'Bow Waste' containers make train identification easy as 66527 *Don Raider* heads along the ECML at Marholm with 6L01,  Port Clarence - Chesterton Junction. (JR)

**JUNE** (cont.)

### Construction Materials

**(1) :** To create space for the new CTRL lines, King's Cross cement terminal closes and a new terminal opens just north of St. Pancras.

Consequently, the Ketton to King's Cross train has been replaced by:

6M85, Ketton - St. Pancras (L)          6E93, St. Pancras - Ketton (E)

The inward flow is routed via the ECML with a run round at Cricklewood and the empties run via the Midland main line and Melton Mowbray.

*Right* : Still sporting black diamond coal sector decals, 60057*Adam Smith* trundles along the 'Down fast' on the Midland main line at Oakley, 3 miles north of Bedford, with the returning 6E93, St. Pancras - Ketton cement empties. (NG)

*Below* : For the record, a panoramic view of the former Castle Cement terminal adjacent to King's Cross goods yard.

As can be seen, the inward working (6M85) was worked by an unidentified locomotive and the train is divided into two portions for operating convenience. Prior to combining the two portions, 66204 sits in readiness for the departure of 6M93, King's Cross - Ketton cement empties. (CB)

**(2) :** A new development in the Peak District is the flow of Lime Mortar powder from RMC's Dove Hole quarry to their receiving terminal at Bletchley, aided by a SRA grant of £518,000 towards the cost of installing new silos and unloading equipment. Refurbished PCA tank wagons will be used for this new flow.

*Right* : Two of these orange liveried PCA tanks are seen at the rear of 6H55, Bletchley - Peak Forest stone empties, passing Cathiron on the WCML near Rugby. (MB)

## JUNE (cont.) : Domestic Waste

To complement the established 'Binliner' services, a new working commences from Dagenham in Essex to a landfill site in Buckinghamshire :

6M80, Dagenham - Calvert (L)                 6L81, Calvert - Dagenham (E)

## Coal

The last train of coal leaves Clipstone Colliery, near Mansfield, with 66201 hauling 7B63, the 09:25 to West Burton Power Station; only Harworth, Thoresby and Welbeck collieries remain open in Nottinghamshire.

What will happen to some of the equipment at Clipstone? The pithead winding gear is the highest in the country and is covered by a preservation order.

*Above* : The winding gear is predominant in this view of Clipstone Colliery and 66250 (the last member of the fleet) heading a rake of MGR wagons forming 6W87, the 06:08 Worksop - Clipstone. (CB)

# FREIGHTMASTER

## THE NATIONAL RAILFREIGHT TIMETABLE

Mark Rawlinson

No. 30
Summer
2003

## JULY

### Intermodal

**(1)** : To expand their 'Intermodal express' network, EWS introduce a new daily service between Hams Hall and Southampton Western Docks:

4Z15, Hams Hall - Southampton W. D.    4Z38, Southampton W. D. - Hams Hall

Due to limited capacity at Western Docks, both trains recess for several hours at Eastleigh. 4Z15 has to wait for 6M16, Western Docks - Crewe car train to leave the docks and 4Z38 must be away before 4Y19, Mountfield - Western Docks Gypsum empties arrive!

**(2)** : To cope with growing traffic to both Daventry and Hams Hall, EWS introduce a twice-daily 'shuttle' between the two terminals, ostensibly conveying traffic to/from Grangemouth and Southampton.:

4P14, Hams Hall - Daventry        4P15, Daventry - Hams Hall

4P16, Hams Hall - Daventry        4P17, Daventry - Hams Hall

### AUGUST : Metals

**(1)** : Under new Spanish ownership (Celsa), the former Allied Steel & Wire works at Cardiff starts to produce steel again. The plant is receiving scrap metal by rail although not yet dispatching steel. Steel production is initially low and rail traffic is limited to a weekly service bringing scrap to the plant from the East Midlands.

The following month sees a doubling of traffic with a new flow emanating from Saltley scrapyard to Cardiff Tidal, which augurs well for the future:

6V97, Beeston  - Cardiff Tidal (L)
6M74, Cardiff Tidal - Beeston (E )

6V24, Washwood Heath - Cardiff  (L)
6M21, Cardiff  - Washwood Heath (E)

*Right* : One of these new scrap metal workings; 6V97, Beeston - Cardiff Tidal, passes Elford on the Derby - Birmingham mainline headed by 66003, substituting for the 'booked' class 60 locomotive. (MB)

**(2)** : An interesting development sees the first 'block' train (excluding automotive and intermodal traffic, etc) through the Channel Tunnel - steel bound for  Ebange in Northern France. The steel can be sourced from either Scunthorpe or Lackenby.

*Right* : Passing Bromham, north of Bedford on the Midland Mainline, 66091 heads 6O25, the 22:03 Scunthorpe - Dollands Moor service running some 5 hours late, thus enabling a daytime pictorial record to be obtained!

What makes this train particularly interesting is that the train (excluding the locomotive) is formed entirely of French rolling stock. (NG)

## AUGUST

### Coal

Having successfully run coal trains for two years, Freightliner Heavy Haul achieve a notable first by running coal trains over the WCML between Carlisle and Crewe for the first time ***AND***, these trains have been allocated a 'proper' (WTT) headcode instead of the more usual 'Z' (Special) reporting numbers. The services are:

| | |
|---|---|
| 6M61, Hunterston - Rugeley power station (L) | 4S41, Rugeley - Hunterston (E) |
| 6M62, Hunterston - Rugeley (L) | 4S42, Rugeley - Hunterston (E) |

To avoid the rather congested GSW route, all trains are routed north of Carlisle via Beattock.

*Above* : Of course, coal flows vary according to the demand of individual power stations and from where the coal is to be sourced. On this occasion, one of these new coal trains ran to Cottam power station and the 'empties' (4S42) are seen approaching Crawford en-route to Ravenstruther with 66527 *Don Raider* providing the traction. (PJR)

### Petroleum

A new petroleum flow starts with fuel oil being conveyed from Teesside to West Burton power station, replacing the previous flow from Lindsey refinery:

| | |
|---|---|
| 6G50, Seal Sands - West Burton (L) | 6G51, West Burton - Seal Sands (E) |

This service will only run for two months before losing out to road transport. However, as a consequence, the old 6D74, Lindsey - Ferrybridge power station fuel oil train is cancelled and replaced by the former Seals Sands flow, routed to Ferrybridge and coded 6G50!

## SEPTEMBER

### Intermodal

A new service, operated by DRS, comes on stream on behalf of their customer W H Malcolm to complement the existing Grangemouth service, but this time linking Daventry with Coatbridge.

| | |
|---|---|
| 4M44, Coatbridge - Daventry | 4S45, Daventry - Coatbridge |

## SEPTEMBER (cont.) Coal

A new MGR coal flow starts running this month from a new source using HAA wagons to West Burton power station, booked for class 60 traction. The trains are routed via Micklefield, Gascoigne Wood, Hambleton, Doncaster, Maltby and Worksop:

7B67, Hunslet - West Burton (L)    6W67, West Burton - Worksop (E), then:

6K67, Worksop - Hunslet (E)

*Above* : A setting sun provides some fine Autumnal lighting as 60001 *The Railway Observer* passes Red Hill, near Tickhill on the South Yorkshire Joint Line, with 7B67, the 13:21 Hunslet - West Burton loaded MGR. (CB)

## Minerals

After months of speculation, class 56's come off the 'Boulby Line' trains conveying Potash and Rock Salt from the Boulby mine to Tees Dock and Middlesbrough Goods, respectively. The trains are now 'booked' for class 60 operation although class 66's will also work these trains.

This change is due to a decision taken by Cleveland Potash and EWS to save money and provide scope for future traffic by increasing the length of each train from 10 to 15 wagons, thus necessitating more powerful motive power to haul these trains over the heavily graded route.

## OCTOBER

### Coal

Only 15 months late!..... Originally planned to take place in July 2002, class 56s finally bow out on the Immingham - Scunthorpe steelworks coal 'shuttles.' EWS have now introduced their HTA coal hoppers on the circuit, which can only be hauled by class 66s.

### Intermodal

Freightliner introduce a new cement service between Earles in the Hope Valley and Selby using 'Piggyback' wagons like those operating between Westbury cement works and Millbrook freightliner terminal, Southampton:

6Z16, Earles - Selby Potter Group (L)    6Z17, Selby - Earles (E)

# FREIGHTMASTER

## THE NATIONAL RAILFREIGHT TIMETABLE

Mark Rawlinson

No. 31
Autumn
2003

## OCTOBER (cont.) : Locomotives

DRS introduce their new class 66/4 locomotives into revenue service on the Anglo-Scottish intermodals, ostensibly replacing pairs of class 37s on the Malcolm traffic.

*Above* : One of the new DRS locomotives (66408) passes Cathiron on the WCML, some 10 miles or so from its destination, heading 4M44, Coatbridge - Daventry intermodal. The locomotive will return to Scotland later in the day on 4S45, Daventry - Coatbridge. (MB)

*Below* : Prior to the introduction of the new locomotives, DRS hire 66710 from GBRf to help out with traction for Anglo-Scottish services; 66710 heads south at Beckfoot with 4M44, the new Coatbridge - Daventry W H Malcolm train which was introduced last month. (RN)

**OCTOBER** (cont.)

### Intermodal / Freightliner

A busy month with several new services coming on stream:

**(1)** : Following on from last month's new DRS / Malcolm / ASDA train from Coatbridge, new services run to Daventry from Mossend (EWS) and Felixstowe (Freightliner). The EWS train is the Mossend to Warrington 'timberliner', extended to Daventry, and is officially an 'Enterprise' service, although only intermodal traffic is usually conveyed south of Warrington:

| | | | |
|---|---|---|---|
| 4M63, Mossend | - Daventry | 4S62, Daventry | - Mossend |
| 4M52, Ipswich Yard | - Daventry | 4Z52, Daventry | - Ipswich Yard |

**(2)** : To complement these services, GB railfreight operate a 'trip' between Daventry and Hams Hall, which is a connection off a new afternoon service:

| | |
|---|---|
| 4M23, Felixstowe - Hams Hall | 4L23, Hams Hall - Felixstowe |

During the week, 4L23 is routed via London and on a Saturday, via Nottingham.

**(3)** : Another new intermodal service links Trafford Park and Teesside, running overnight via Diggle:

4M54, Tees Dock - Trafford Park

4E54, Trafford Park - Tees Dock

**(4)** : The EWS intermodal network is further extended, this time to North Humberside with a weekly flow of containerised steel from Scunthorpe steelworks bound for export .

6L02, (FO) Scunthorpe - Felixstowe (L)

6A12, (SO) Felixstowe - Harwich (E)

6Z26, (MO) Harwich - Scunthorpe (E)

*Right* : The Scunthorpe intermodal can easily be distinguished by a consist of 'Evergreen' or 'Cosco' containers. On this occasion, 6Z26 from Harwich approaches Frodingham, Scunthorpe, with 66145 hauling mostly Cosco containers.

This flow of steel can also be exported via the ports of Immingham and Grain (Thamesport). (MB)

### NOVEMBER : Construction Materials

**(1)** : In conjunction with the Heathrow Terminal 5 project, a new dedicated EWS service is introduced bringing steel rods to the site. As construction gathers pace, additional flows of steel will commence from other sources, such as Cardiff Tidal.

| | |
|---|---|
| 6V85, Chatham Docks - Colnbrook (L) | 6O82, Colnbrook - Hoo Junction (E) |

**(2)** : Freightliner take delivery of their new MJA bogie box wagons for use on the Port Clarence traffic and aggregate trains between Tower (South Wales) and Harlow Mill (Essex). Of interest, is that the wagons are permanently coupled in pairs.

**(3)** : After months of problems, Gypsum and Limestone trains finally start running to the new Gas Flue Desulpherisation (GFD) plant at West Burton power station. The trains are operated by GBRf and EWS, respectively:

| | |
|---|---|
| 4O20, West Burton - Mountfield (L) | 4E20, Mountfield - West Burton (E) |
| 6E56, Tunstead - West Burton (L) | 6M96, West Burton - Tunstead (E) |

*Above* : Sweeping round the curve on the approach to East Usk, Newport, 66607 heads a rake of the new  MJA box wagons returning empty to South Wales from Essex, forming 6V55, Dagenham - Tower.  (MB)

*Below* : The new  GBRf Gypsum service from West Burton to Mountfield (4O20) crew changes at Peterborough and, having arrived some two hours earlier, the train is seen making its way out of Peterborough Yard  at the 'booked' time of 10:10hrs. The train engine is 'Bluebird' 66714 *Cromer Lifeboat* passing Eastfield signalbox; a 'box' retained when Peterborough was resignalled in the 1970's to control access to the 'up' sidings. (MB)

# FREIGHTMASTER

## THE NATIONAL RAILFREIGHT TIMETABLE

Mark Rawlinson

No. 32
Winter
2004

## JANUARY

### Mail

This month sees the final runs of the Royal Mail's Travelling Post Office (TPO) trains, ending 166 years of railway history. The last trains ran during the 9th & 10th of January and involve 9 trains: 4 services to / from Low Fell (Newcastle), 2 to / from Carlisle and 4 to / from Plymouth / Penzance. The details of the final runs are:

| | | | | | |
|---|---|---|---|---|---|
| 67021 | 1E94, | 22:15 | Bristol Parkway | - | Low Fell |
| 67023 | 1V28, | 20:24 | Low Fell | - | Bristol Parkway |
| 90033 | 1E53, | 23:12 | Willesden | - | Low Fell |
| 90037 | 1M91, | 20:48 | Low Fell | - | Willesden |
| 90029 | 1A93, | 21:18 | Carlisle | - | Willesden |
| 90024 | 1C00, | 23:18 | Willesden | - | Carlisle |
| 67025 | 1M99, | 22:11 | Plymouth | - | Willesden |
| 67026 | 1V40, | 23:10 | Willesden | - | Plymouth |
| 67007 | 1C01, | 19:35 | Penzance | - | Bristol Parkway |
| 67007 | 1C02, | 00:55 | Bristol Parkway | - | Penzance |

*Top Right* : All mail that is posted on a TPO is franked using a special handstamp, which distinguishes on which TPO a letter is posted. These two handstamps are a record of mail posted on the last 'North West' TPO services:

    North West 'Up'    : 1A93        North West 'Down' : 1C00

*Below* : The last Friday night of operation features unprecedented public interest, just to either post letters for special handstamps or to witness the end of another era of rail history. At Exeter St. Davids, 67007 waits to depart with the last 'up' Cornish TPO (1C01) suitably adorned with headboard. (DM)

**JANUARY** (cont.)

### Construction Materials

**(1)** : EWS is awarded a 'one off' contract to move over 200,000 tonnes of stone from RMC's Dove Holes Quarry in Derbyshire to Acton Yard for the redevelopment of White City in West London. Mendip Rail 101-tonne hopper wagons will be used to convey the aggregate and Foster Yeoman will handle and store the aggregate before delivering to the concrete batching plants operated by RMC Readymix on site.

The contract should last about 18-20 months and involves an out & back working, thus:

6V58, Peak Forest - Acton Yard (L)

6M34, Acton Yard - Peak Forest (E)

*Right*: This new working is particularly noteworthy on two counts: the use of Mendip Rail (Hanson / Foster Yeoman) hopper wagons for stone sourced at Peak Forest and the sight of such wagons on the Midland main line!

EWS liveried 60010 is seen passing Oakley on the Midland main line in charge of 6M34, Acton Yard - Peak Forest stone empties. (NG)

**(2)** : Work begins on the dualling of the main line in Cornwall between Burngullow and Probus with ballast being brought in from Meldon Quarry.

6F95, Meldon Quarry - St. Blazey (L)          6F94, St. Blazey - Meldon Quarry (E)

*Above* : It's 22 months since the previous ballast from the quarry! Passing Gunstone Mill, between Crediton and Yeoford, 37308 + 37047 head 6G94, the 08:50 St. Blazey - Meldon empties, comprising 10 MRA wagons and 4 Seacows. (DM)

### JANUARY (cont.) : **Automotive**

The first train to use the new Freightliner Heavy Haul covered Autoflats ('Autoliner') runs on 21st. January from Portbury Docks, forming 6S41 to Mossend. The load is six Autoflats and four TAL wagons, carrying Fiat, Lexus, Mitsubishi and Toyota vehicles.

*Top* : This excellent illustration depicts some new Freightliner 'Autoflats' in the formation of the 17:50 Portbury - Mossend (coded 6X42 'out of gauge'), comprising 4 twin cartics and 7 twin 'Autoliners'.

This particular service is routed via the 'Marches' route to Crewe, thence the WCML to Mossend. Upon leaving Newport for Caerleon, 66561 is seen crossing the bridge spanning the River Usk (actually called St. Julians Viaduct); Newport Transporter Bridge and Uskmouth 'B' Power Station are both visible in the background. (AK)

### FEBRUARY : **Intermodal**

EWS secure a contract from Argos to move supplies between London and Burton-on-Trent and means yet another new location to add to the intermodal network:

4P20, Willesden - Burton-on-Trent

4P21, Burton    - Willesden

*Right* : The consist of 4P21 is a rake of container flats as 66198 passes Kingsbury en-route to Willesden with a class 60 waiting in the background to work 6E59, Kingsbury - Lindsey empty bogie tanks. (MB)

**FEBRUARY** (cont.)

### Construction Materials

Two new flows commence this month, operated by Freightliner on behalf of Lafarge, which break new ground in the process. The first sees cement trains running over the Settle & Carlisle for the first time in more than 20 years, albeit bagged cement in cargowaggons, and the second sees cement tanks running over the northern section of the WCML via Beattock:

6M38,  Earles Sidings  - Brunthill  (L)         6M39,  Brunthill - Earles Sidings (E)

6M01,  Oxwellmains    - Brunthill (L)         6S09,   Brunthill - Oxwellmains (E)

In fact, 2004 shapes up to be the year of cement with further new freight flows coming on stream.

British Lime Industries (Cement) award EWS a seven year contract to move cement by rail from it's new £115 million cement works at Tunstead Quarry, which will remove 24,000 lorry movements and 4.5 million lorry kilometres from the road network each year. The services are:

6M09,  Tunstead - Walsall (L)              6M82,  Walsall - Tunstead (E)

6E28,  Tunstead - Leeds Hunslet (L)        6M22,  Hunslet - Tunstead (E)

In August, a new terminal is to open at Theale, near Reading, on the site of the original Blue Circle depot which was demolished 15 years ago, with services operated by Freightliner on behalf of Lafarge. The new trains will be routed via the Midland Main Line and will probably increase in frequency once the terminal is fully up and running:

6V91,  Earles - Theale (L)                 6M91,  Theale - Earles (E)

*Above* : A visit to the new cement terminal at Walsall Tasker Street enables the photographer to record 60023 in attendance, prior to departing with 6M82, Walsall - Tunstead empty cement tanks. (RN)

*Above* : The flow of cement from Earles to Carlisle Brunthill uses Ferrywagons to convey bagged cement as we can see here in this view of 66601 passing Armathwaite with 6M39, Brunthill - Earles empty cement vans. (PJR)

*Below* : The new Kingstown Railfreight Terminal comprises Carlisle warehousing and the Lafarge cement depot, which is located at Brunthill on the truncated ex-Waverley Route. At the terminal, 66615 waits for its PCA tanks to be discharged in order to return with the 6S09 service to Oxwellmains. (DMc)

## MARCH

### Automotive

After a two year absence, the flow of Nissan cars from Tyne Dock to Dollands Moor resumes and, since through trains to the continent began in 1999, this flow has been intermittent. The original flow used the 'WIA' enclosed car carriers, but these have since been redeployed to Jaguar traffic, so the new Nissan flow uses open cartics, hence an 'X' (out of gauge) headcode:

6X19, Tyne Dock - Dollands Moor (L)

The empties return by 'scheduled' services including 6X38, Washwood Heath - Bathgate.

### Construction Materials

The long-awaited Merehead to Chichester stone flow starts with, perhaps rather surprisingly, both the loaded and empty trains routed via the St.Denys to Fareham (via Hamble) line.

7O52, Merehead - Chichester  (L)            7V18, Chichester - Merehead (E)

### Minerals

A new flow sees additional traffic to Goole Docks in the form of industrial sand from East Anglia. This is a 5 year contract awarded by WBB Minerals to EWS to move 130,000 tonnes a year from Leziate Quarry, near Kings Lynn, to a brand new Guardian glass works in Goole.

The new service runs as:

6E88,  Middleton Towers - Peterborough (L)    6H92, Peterborough - Goole (L)

6H93,  Goole            - Peterborough (E)    6L98,  Peterborough - Middleton Towers (E)

*Above* : Passing Peterborough at the correct time, 66075 heads along the 'Up' slow line with empty sand hoppers, running on this particular occasion as 6L98, the 07:33 Worksop Yard - Middleton Towers. To the right of the last sand hopper, is the GB Railfreight depot yard, where some class 66/7 locomotives can be seen stabled. The building above the locomotive is a home for young offenders detained at Her Majesty's pleasure. (MB)

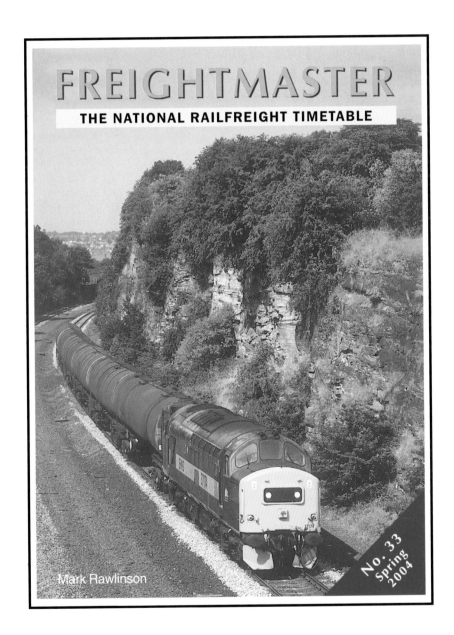

# FREIGHTMASTER

## THE NATIONAL RAILFREIGHT TIMETABLE

No. 33 Spring 2004

Mark Rawlinson

## APRIL

### Operations

**(1)** : It is announced that coal production is to cease at the largest coal mining complex in the UK, Gascoigne Wood.

In fact, 66552 *Maltby Raider* has the distinction of working the last officially booked train to load from Gascoigne Wood before the mine closes by UK Coal on 12 November 2004.

**(2)** : Also, the remaining class 56 locomotives are all withdrawn from traffic after 28 years of active service. Great shame!

*Right* : A once familiar sight at Milford Junction, which will now be consigned to history. On an overcast day, 56025 hurries along the 'up Normanton' with 6M79, Redcar - Clitheroe loaded MEA wagons and past 66220 on 6H16, the 12:50 Gascoigne Wood - Drax loaded EWS hoppers. (MB)

**(3)** : Some good news! ........ Whitemoor Yard comes back to life ..... from being once the largest marshalling yard in Europe, to total dereliction for ten years, Whitemoor is now back in business as one of Network Rail's largest infrastructure yards. To commemorate the occasion, GB Railfreight locomotive No. 66701 is re-named *Whitemoor*.

Consequently, Temple Mills yard will close with the transfer of Network Rail's Peterborough site to the new yard, thus eliminating its virtual quarry. The Tallington 'trip' to Tarmac's concrete sleeper works will also run to Whitemoor instead of Peterborough.

*Above* : This is the scene at Whitemoor Junction during construction of the new yard with an ex-BR Class 14 shunting locomotive waiting to enter the yard and 67024 preparing to leave with 6Z23 to Peterborough. The line leading into the distance above the class 67 is the disused branch to Wisbech. (JR)

**APRIL** (cont.) **: Intermodal**

**(1) :** EWS withdraw their Ditton to Felixstowe intermodal service (4L72 / 4M43) and replace it with a new service from Wembley to Felixstowe South via Ely (Potter Group) and a complicated trainplan; interestingly, 4Z74 and 4Z75 are routed via Royston and Hitchin:

| | | |
|---|---|---|
| 4Z74, | Wembley | - Ely |
| 4Z75, | Ely | - Wembley |
| | | |
| 4Z25, | Harwich | - Felixstowe |
| 4Z26, | Felixstowe | - Ely |
| 4Z27, | Ely | - Harwich |

*Top Right* : One of the spare class 67 locomotives (67001) has been commandeered to work one of these new EWS intermodal services: 4Z74, the 09:55 Wembley - Ely Papworth, photographed approaching Royston. Apart from engineers trains and the seasonal 'Water Cannons', these intermodals are the only freight services to traverse the 26-mile long Hitchin - Royston - Cambridge line. (NG)

**(2) :** After numerous false alarms, the DRS / Malcolm / Asda train from Grangemouth to Aberdeen finally starts but, due limited pathing on the Dundee to Aberdeen line, the southbound train runs in the path of Freightliner's empty cement train on days when the latter is not running:

    4A11, Grangemouth - Aberdeen           4N83, Aberdeen - Grangemouth

*Above* : The introduction of the new DRS service makes a colourful sight on the northern stretches of the Aberdeen main line with a combination of blue (Malcolm) and green & white (ASDA) containers. The colourful ensemble is passing Carmont, near Stonehaven, with 66406 heading 6N83, the 17:30 Aberdeen Guild Street - Grangemouth. Carmont being a popular location for railway photographers, plus the added delight of semaphore signalling! (PJR)

### APRIL (cont.) **Freightliner**

It's a landmark month for the Port of Felixstowe, the UK's largest container port, with the number of containers being transported through the port by rail reaching an all-time high. Towards the end of the month, the weekly total smashes through the 7,000 barrier (7,006 containers to be precise) at a staggering daily average in excess of 1,000; breaking the previous record by some 330 units set in December 2003.

There are now 22 inbound / 21 outbound trains per day from the North and South terminals, serving Birmingham (Lawley St.), Cardiff, Cleveland (Wilton), Coatbridge, Daventry, Hams Hall, Leeds, Liverpool (Garston), Manchester (Trafford Park), Selby, Tilbury and Widnes. The Port also handles two forest products trains per day at its dedicated paper-handling rail terminal.

Two contrasting views of Felixstowe. A panoramic view of the Port *(Above)* shows several ships birthed, most heavily laden with containers. In fact, Felixstowe can handle the largest container ships in the world like, for example, the Maersk Sealand *MV. Arnold Maersk* - 352 metres long, 93,496 gross tonnes and capable of carrying 6,600 TEUs (20-feet Equivalent Units, which is the term in which container volumes are measured!). Meanwhile, at the container terminal, 57007 *Freightliner Bond (Below)* waits for the final containers to be loaded in readiness for its departure to Ipswich Yard, thence going forward as the 4S88 service to Coatbridge. (Both MB)

# FREIGHTMASTER

## THE NATIONAL RAILFREIGHT TIMETABLE

No. 34
Summer
2004

Mark Rawlinson

66708

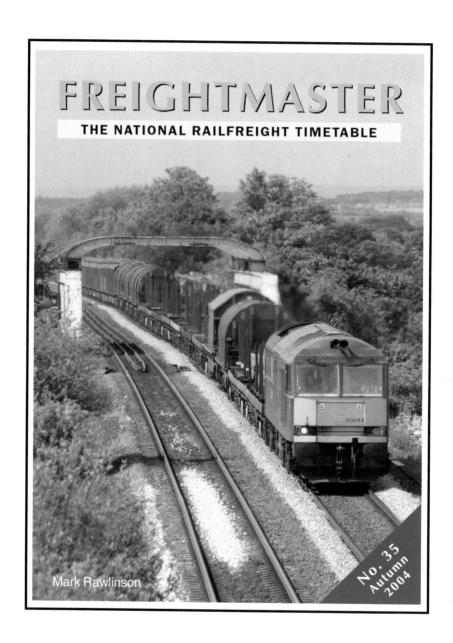

# FREIGHTMASTER

## THE NATIONAL RAILFREIGHT TIMETABLE

60044

Mark Rawlinson

No. 35
Autumn
2004

## OCTOBER : Construction Materials

Freightliner continue to expand their aggregate business with a new flow of stone (emanating for the first time from Peak Forest) to Hitchin using FHH box wagons. Of further note, the existing Tower - Dagenham flow (6L04 / 6V55) is now being sourced from Moreton-on-Lugg.

6E99, Peak Forest - Hitchin (L)

6E57, Hitchin - Barrow Hill (E)

6M35, Barrow Hill - Peak Forest (E)

## NOVEMBER : Intermodal

**(1)** : EWS temporarily suspend the majority of their intermodal services due to customers voicing concern about their needs not being met in light of the threat of industrial action.

**(2)** : DRS launch a new Scottish intermodal service between Grangemouth and Elderslie (near Paisley) with both trains routed via Cumbernauld, Coatbridge and Rutherglen. The first train is rather surprisingly worked by a class 37 locomotive and not by one of DRS's newer class 66 locomotives!

4Z77, Grangemouth - Elderslie

4Z78, Elderslie - Grangemouth

*Right* : One of these new intermodals is seen passing Greenhill Lower Junction, with 37259 heading for Elderslie with a short rake of containers forming 4Z77 ex-Grangemouth. (IL)

## DECEMBER : Mail

Some great news to end the year and my Review .... mail trains return to the rail network, albeit on a trial basis until March 2005, using Royal Mail's class 325 units driven by GB Railfreight traincrew. In addition to the scheduled services listed below, there will be two further trains during December (1Z11 / 1Z14) between Willesden and Shieldmuir to handle the 'Christmas Peak':

1S96, 15:44 Willesden - Shieldmuir

1Z16, 15:32 Shieldmuir - Warrington

1A97, 20:28 Warrington - Willesden

*Above* : One of the 'Christmas Peak' additional mail services makes for a colourful sight near Penrith, as three 325 units (325003 / 325001 / 3250008) head south forming 1Z14, the 10:28 Shieldmuir - Willesden PRDC. (PJR)

# RAILFREIGHT MISCELLANY

Although this Review concentrates on freight developments between 1995 - 2004, it is important to reiterate the importance of the 'run of the mill' freight flows which do not get a mention, pre-date FREIGHTMASTER and are still running today. Examples include petroleum from Humberside to Kingsbury, steel products from Margam to Round Oak, lime from Hardendale to Redcar, etc, - regular scheduled services contributing to a healthy railfreight sector.

In addition, there are many other freight services which do not survive beyond initial trials or run for specific 'one-off' events / very short term contracts and a small selection (along with a few other bits & pieces) are featured here for the record!

### Automotive :

During 2002 / 2003, 4M26, Dagenham - Crewe Gresty Lane Ford car / van train takes advantage of a spare path on the Midland Mainline, thus providing Freightliner drivers with valuable route knowledge over the southern section of the former Midland Route.

*Right* : The train is frequently worked by a class 47 locomotive, as we see here. XP64 liveried 47853 *Rail Express,* negotiates the curves to the south of Wellingborough with 4M26 bound for Crewe and a trainload of transit vans. (JR)

### Freightliner :

As a result of the 'Mad Cow' disease epidemic in 2001, burned carcasses were moved by rail in containers for internment at the landfill site at Calvert.

*Above* : A rare working indeed, freight on the Chiltern Line! 66518 hauls 'Cow Ash' containers through Quainton Road station on 4Z71, the 08:00 Crewe Basford Hall - Calvert. (BM)

## Associated British Ports (ABP) :

During this Review, British ports see a significant increase in railfreight activity, especially smaller ports like Grangemouth, Tees Dock, Tyne Dock and those in South Wales.

*Right* : This panoramic view depicts 56100 leaving Tyne Dock in October 1999 with the first of three trains of Taiwanese steel for Wolverhampton Steel Terminal, conveyed in telescopic steel containers.

Not only does this picture illustrate the docks complex, it is also a good example of a 'very' Short Term working! (PJR)

## Coal :

You're right, just another coal train! But, having already featured some of the longest MGR coal flows in the country, I thought it fitting to feature the shortest.

One or two trains run each weekday from Redcar Coal terminal to Wilton, which is a round trip of under 5 miles.

*Right* : The short journey is not so straightforward as a reversal at Grangetown is required. After running round its train of loaded coal on the 'down goods' line adjacent to Grangetown signalbox, 66042 heads for Wilton with 6N34, the 08:30 Redcar - Wilton. (MB)

## Pipes :

EWS often run intense short-term traffic flows for Corus, moving both 20 inch and 42 inch pipes from it's Hartlepool works for North Sea oil industry use and other construction projects.

*Right* : A popular freight service with photographers is the movement of pipes from Hartlepool to Georgemas Junction. 37517 + 37682 *Hartlepool Pipe Mill* approach Bridge of Earn with 6X88, the 07:30 Hartlepool Pipe Mill - Georgemas Junction. All these trains are coded (X) 'out of gauge'. (PJR)

**Intermodal** :

**August 1999**:

On 11 August 1999, the UK witnesses a total eclipse of the sun, which attracts thousands of extra visitors to Cornwall to see the event. In association with this, EWS run special trains to the West Country bringing in refrigeration units and bottled water.

*Right* : Passing Dawlish Warren, 66010 hauls 6V42, Southampton Millbrook - Tavistock Junction refrigerated containers for use in Cornish supermarkets to provide additional capacity in expectation of large crowds for the total solar eclipse. (DM)

**October 1999**

Two years after the unsuccessful Penrith - Cricklewood 'milkliner', another trial is run by EWS between Yeovil and Willesden.

Although the trial is considered a success, no further business materialises. Perhaps, with more courage and a will to succeed among respective parties, projects like this would come to fruition.

*Right* : On 5 October 1999, 66017 stands in the yard at Yeovil Pen Mill whilst milk is being transferred from a lorry to the sole milk tank on the train, which will form 4Z18, the 18:30 service to Willesden. (DM)

**September 2002**

EWS stage the first non-stop 90mph freight trial on the 24th. on the WCML using FIA wagons and empty P & O Nedlloyd containers.

The trial runs as 3S00, Wembley - Mossend, returning as 3S01 to Wembley the following day. If Network Rail can provide paths, this speed improvement will open up more opportunities to increase traffic at the expense of lorries......

*Right* : The 3S00, 10:15 Wembley - Mossend 90mph trial passes through Tamworth Low Level station hauled by 90034. (RN)

### 'Enterprise' :

The 'Enterprise' network is ideally placed to transport 'ad-hoc' wagonload materials in addition to regular commodities, as and when required.

*Right* : On one occasion in October 1997, the payload of 6C46, St. Blazey - Newport ADJ 'Enterprise', consists entirely of shot blast debris from Falmouth Docks.

The train is unusually formed of Greater Manchester waste containers and hauled by the equally unusual combination of 60093 *Jack Stirk* + 37671 *Tre Pol and Pen* seen passing Rewe. (DM)

### Freight Multiple Unit (MPV) :

Any innovation and competition which encourage alternative methods of railfreight is backed by the Government. However, the trial of the MPV has not got off the ground despite two sets of trials in 2000 and 2001.

*Right* : MPV's DR98904 and DR98906 reverse into the yard at Hereford in order to gain access to the Bulmers branch. The train, 6Z79, Willesden - Hereford, is formed of four 45ft. 'Seaco' containers. Note, a normal MPV uses a power car and trailer or non powered vehicle, but this trial uses 2 powered vehicles. (AK)

### Ministry of Defence (MoD) :

In addition to scheduled timetabled services, EWS run 'special' trains for the MoD in connection with military exercises and the large-scale movement of equipment.

*Right* : One such exercise takes place necessitating a special train to convey traffic to Sennybridge in April 2000.

The train is pictured reversing up into the old Celtic Energy coal loading terminal at Cwmbargoed to be offloaded. The 'special' is 6Z86, the 14:08 Margam - Cwmbargoed hauled by 60041. (AK)

# HEADCODES

A 'Headcode' is used by National Rail to keep track of trains. The full train identification, used by the operators TOPS Computer, actually consists of ten characters but, in everyday use, only four are used:

So, let's examine the component parts of a working headcode:

The <u>first character</u> denotes the train type:

**0** = Light Engine

**1** = Mail/TPO (express passenger)

**2** = Stopping Passenger Train

**3** = 90 m.p.h. freight

**4** = 75 m.p.h. freight

**5** =  Empty mail vans (coaching stock)

**6** = 60 m.p.h. freight

**7** = 45 m.p.h. freight

**8** = 35 m.p.h. freight

**9** = International passenger services

The <u>second character</u> represents the destination area:

**A** : London & Home counties / Aberdeen

**B** : South Wales / Southampton / Rugby - Bletchley / Edinburgh

**C** : Carlisle / Bristol + South West England

**D** : Toton + Mountsorrel / Glasgow / North Wales
Doncaster + most of Yorkshire & Humberside

**E** : Inter regional to **E**astern

**F** : Warrington + Liverpool area / Leicester area

**G** : West Midlands / Fife / STP workings (within Eastern / Western regions)

**H** : Peterborough / Manchester (south) / Inverness + Far North

 **I** : (not used)

**J** : Chirk / Manchester (north)

**K** : Crewe + Stoke

**L** : Inter regional to Ang**L**ia

**M** : Inter regional to **M**idland

**N** : Newcastle + Teesside / Grangemouth

**O** : Inter regional to **S**outhern

**P** : STP workings (within Midland region)

**Q** : (not used)

**R** : Felixstowe Branch / Ayrshire

**S** : Inter regional to **S**cotland

**T** : (not used) - but certain engineers trains

**U** : Local trains within North Kent

**V** : Inter regional to **W**estern

**W** : Dorset

**X** : 'Out of gauge' loads (cars, pipes, etc)

**Y** : Trains within Southern Region / Ipswich / West Highland

**Z** : STP workings, except those within Eastern / LMR / Western regions

The last two characters identify the particular train: eg: 6V27, 4M16, etc.

So, by way of example, headcode 4M30 represents a 75 m.p.h. freight train, travelling to the Midland region, number 30; in fact, the DRS operated 19:15 Grangemouth - Daventry, intermodal service.

*NOTES* :

1. special codes apply to trains between Dollands Moor and Wembley / Willesden.

2. most power station coal trains have their own codes:

   **A** : loads to Ratcliffe / empties from Drax to Gascoigne Wood

   **B** : loads to West Burton .

   **C** : loads to Eggborough / empties from Aire Valley to Immingham

   **D** : loads from Avonmouth to Didcot and empties v.v.

   **F** : Ferrybridge (low numbers) + Cottam (high numbers)

   **G** : all English FHH coal trains & empties, regardless of power station

   **H** : loads to Drax (cannot be 'D', as WTT trains in the area are 'D') / empties from Bescot + Washwood Heath to Daw Mill

   **J** : empties to Hunterston

   **K** : empties from Worksop

   **P** : empties to Toton (STP only - WTT trains use 'D')

   **R** : empties from Knottingley / Sudforth to Gascoigne Wood

   **T** : empties from Toton

   **U** : Anglo-Scottish coal trains to Drax

   **W** : empties to Worksop

   **Y** : empties from Knottingley/Drax

Other power stations use 'proper' headcodes (e.g. Aberthaw uses 'B' / Rugeley 'G')

3. Freightliner trains to / from Felixstowe South use 'B' instead of 'R'.

4. Scunthorpe Iron Ore / coal: Iron ore use 'T' (loaded) / 'K' (empty) instead of 'D'
   
   Coal use 'C' (loaded + empty) instead of 'D'

# 'ENTERPRISE'

Transrail launch their 'Enterprise' network in October 1994 and the initial services are:

6S44, Willesden - Mossend        6M27, Mossend - Warrington
     (both trains serve Bescot and Warrington Arpley)

6A15, Mossend - Aberdeen        6D52, Aberdeen - Mossend

6H55, Aberdeen - Inverness
     (serves Elgin, Huntly and Inverurie)

6H51, Inverness - Elgin        6A16, Elgin - Aberdeen

6R02, Mossend - Mossend
     ('Trip' serving Dalry)

6D30, Mossend - Deanside        6D31, Deanside - Mossend

6G10, Mossend - Cameron Bridge        6D10, Cameron Bridge - Mossend
     (both trains serve Thornton)

6A37, Mossend - Aberdeen        6D03, Aberdeen - Mossend
     (6A37 serves Millerhill)

7Y39, Mossend - Fort William        7D19, Fort William - Mossend
     (both trains serve Coatbridge and Corpach)

6H69, Warrington Arpley - Trafford Park        6F69, Trafford Park - Warrington Arpley
     (both trains serve Guide Bridge)

6F39, Warrington - Dee Marsh        6F46, Dee Marsh - Warrington

6T67, Warrington - Warrington
     ('Trip' serving Ditton and Runcorn)

6T68, Warrington - Warrington
     ('Trip' serving Castleton, Ince UKF, Middlewich, Sandbach and St. Helens)

6C15, Warrington - Workington        6F47, Workington - Warrington
     (6C15 serves Carlisle Yard and Sellafield)

6E32, Warrington - Tees Yard        6M26, Tees Yard - Warrington
     (both trains serve Haverton Hil, Middlesborough Goods and Port Clarence)

6O76, Willesden - Sheerness        6M87, Sheerness - Willesden
     (both trains serve Sittingbourne)

6OO1, Willesden - Quidhampton        6M73, Quidhampton - Willesden

6B10, Newport ADJ - Swansea Burrows        6B14, Swansea Burrows - Newport ADJ

6M24, Newport ADJ - Bescot        6V35, Bescot - Newport ADJ

6T42, Bescot - Bescot
     ('Trip' serving Coleshill and Washwood Heath)

6M72, St. Blazey - Cliffe Vale        6V70, Cliffe Vale - St. Blazey
     (both trains serve Exeter Riverside and Tavistock Junction)

# FREIGHTLINER

This is a typical schedule of Freightliner trains to/from British ports at the time RfD sold its Freightliner division to a management buy-out in May 1996; it should be noted there are also internal freightliner services which operate between inland terminals in the UK.

## SOUTHAMPTON (Maritime & Millbrook)

| Time | Code | Origin |
|---|---|---|
| **Arrivals** | | |
| 0134 MX | 4O07 | Leeds |
| 0354 MX | 4O08 | Trafford Park |
| 0602 MO | 4O09 | Ripple Lane |
| 0605 MX | 4O11 | Garston |
| 0641 MSX | 4O09 | Ripple Lane |
| 0653 SO | 4O09 | Ripple Lane |
| 0811 SO | 4O18 | Lawley Street |
| 0848 MSX | 4O18 | Lawley Street |
| 1105 MX | 4O21 | Garston |
| 1137 SO | 4O22 | Trafford Park |
| 1210 MSX | 4O22 | Trafford Park |
| 1720 EWD | 4O25 | Ripple Lane |
| 1810 SO | 4O26 | Lawley Street |
| 1828 MX | 4O27 | Coatbridge |
| 2100 SO | 4O30 | Trafford Park |
| 2145 SO | 4O32 | Coatbridge |
| 2224 SO | 4O27 | Coatbridge |
| 2240 SO | 4O31 | Leeds |
| **Departures** | | |
| 0320 EWD | 4M95 | Crewe |
| 0510 SO | 4L62 | Ripple Lane |
| 0800 SX | 4L66 | Ripple Lane |
| 0900 SX | 4S55 | Coatbridge |
| 1303 SX | 4S59 | Coatbridge |
| 1310 SO | 4M60 | Lawley Street |
| 1716 SX | 4M99 | Trafford Park |
| 1820 SuO | 4S59 | Coatbridge |
| 1948 SX | 4E76 | Leeds |
| 2013 SX | 4M40 | Crewe |
| 2112 SuO | 4L78 | Ripple Lane |
| 2122 SX | 4M79 | Lawley Street |
| 2207 SX | 4L78 | Ripple Lane |
| 2218 SuO | 4E76 | Leeds |
| 2304 SuO | 4M58 | Trafford Park |
| 2311 SX | 4M58 | Trafford Park |

## FELIXSTOWE (North & South)

| Time | Code | Origin |
|---|---|---|
| **Arrivals** | | |
| 0127 MX | 4L79 | Wilton |
| 0324 MX | 4L60 | Coatbridge |
| 0406 MX | 4L71 | Garston |
| 0617 EWD | 4L82 | Trafford Park |
| 0703 EWD | 4L69 | Lawley Street |
| 0813 EWD | 4L58 | Coatbridge |
| 0959 EWD | 4L95 | Coatbridge |
| 1200 SO | 4L89 | Leeds |
| 1356 MSX | 4L89 | Leeds |
| 1600 EWD | 4L93 | Crewe |
| **Departures** | | |
| 0229 MX | 4M45 | Trafford Park |
| 0821 SX | 4S87 | Coatbridge |
| 1120 SX | 4M47 | Garston |
| 1651 SX | 4S88 | Coatbridge |
| 1732 SX | 4E50 | Wilton |
| 1819 SX | 4M92 | Lawley Street |
| 2042 SX | 4M87 | Trafford Park |
| 2225 SX | 4M73 | Garston |
| 2308 MX | 4R50 | Dagenham |

## TILBURY

| Time | Code | Origin |
|---|---|---|
| **Arrivals** | | |
| 0149 MX | 4L63 | Leeds |
| 0246 MX | 4L98 | Trafford Park |
| 0438 MX | 4L81 | Coatbridge |
| 0854 SO | 4L91 | Crewe |
| 1103 MSX | 4L91 | Crewe |
| 2102 SX | 4L87 | Swindon |
| **Departures** | | |
| 1221 SX | 4M54 | Crewe |
| 1347 SX | 4V15 | Swindon |
| 1830 SX | 4S83 | Coatbridge |
| 2041 SX | 4M37 | Garston |
| 2330 SX | 4E65 | Leeds |

## LIVERPOOL (Seaforth)

| Time | Code | Origin |
|---|---|---|
| **Arrivals** | | |
| 0240 MX | 4F20 | Crewe |
| 0616 MX | 4M81 | Coatbridge |
| **Departures** | | |
| 1126 SO | 4K53 | Crewe |
| 1426 MX | 4K58 | Crewe |
| 1850 MX | 4K69 | Crewe |

## THAMESPORT (Grain)

| Time | Code | Origin |
|---|---|---|
| **Arrivals** | | |
| 0715 MX | 4O84 | Trafford Park |
| 1351 SO | 4O86 | Crewe |
| 1357 MSX | 4O86 | Crewe |
| **Departures** | | |
| 1734 SX | 4M49 | Crewe |
| 1937 SX | 4M96 | Trafford Park |

# ACKNOWLEDGEMENTS

I would like to accord my thanks to the people who have kindly contributed their excellent material for inclusion in this book; without which this title would not have been possible. A full list of contributors is listed below, plus a note of their initials which have been used for accreditation purposes in all supporting captions.

| | | | | | |
|---|---|---|---|---|---|
| Chris Booth | (CB) | Martin Buck | (MB) | Nigel Gibbs | (NG) |
| Adrian Kenny | (AK) | Ian Lothian | (IL) | Dave McAlone | (DMc) |
| Dave Mitchell | (DM) | Brian Morrison | (BM) | Rich Norris | (RN) |
| Peter J Robinson | (PJR) | John Rudd | (JR) | Iain Scotchman | (IS) |
| Paul Shannon | (PS) | | | | |

All maps reproduced, courtesy Mark Rawlinson   (MR)

This is a summary of the Freightmaster 'front cover' illustrations along with other non-captioned photographs included in this book; all by the author unless otherwise stated:

| Page | Loco. | Train Details | | | Location | |
|---|---|---|---|---|---|---|
| 2 | 56018 | 6N32 | Lackenby | - Tees Yard | Tees Yard | |
| 13 | | | Freight Company Logos | | | (MR) |
| 22 | | | Freight Company Logos | | | (MR) |
| 26 | | | Freight Company Logos | | | (MR) |
| 33 | 47229 | 6M03, | Swindon | - Longbridge | Highworth Jct, Swindon | |
| 37 | 37706 | 6V14, | Hull Saltend | - Baglan Bay | East Usk, Newport | |
| 44 | 31407 | 6F11, | Penmaenmawr | - Warrington | Llanddulas | |
| | 31308 | | | | | |
| 54 | 56090 | 6P83, | Middlesbrough | - Boulby | Cargo Fleet | |
| 58 | 60049 | 6V13, | Furzebrook | - Hallen Marsh | Narroways Hill Jct. | |
| 62 | 47060 | 4M99, | Southampton | - Trafford Park | Kings Sutton | |
| 68 | 86241 | 5F91, | Euston D.C.S. | - Warrington | Rugby | |
| 71 | 37706 | 6E21, | Baglan Bay | - Humber | Briton Ferry | |
| 74 | 58014 | 4C13, | Calvert | - Bristol Barrow Road | North Somerset Jct. | |
| 76 | 92024 | 4M74, | Mossend | - Wembley | Greenholme | |
| 77 | 60045 | 6H60, | Hope Street | - Peak Forest | New Mills Jct. | (MR) |
| 85 | 67003 | 1V33, | Willesden | - Plymouth | Stoke Gifford East | |
| 91 | 59201 | 7O66, | Acton Yard | - Angerstein | Wandsworth Road | |
| 97 | 60010 | 6N20, | Scunthorpe | - Tees Yard | Hatfield & Stainforth | |
| 101 | 66604 | 6M16, | Southampton W.D.- | Garston | Basingstoke | |
| 104 | 60007 | 6C65, | Didcot | - Avonmouth | Milton, Didcot | |
| 106 | 37667 | 6D65, | Doncaster | - Immingham | Barnetby | |
| 110 | 66163 | 6Z27, | Ayr | - Ironbridge | Beckfoot | |
| 113 | 66701 | 6L72, | Hams Hall | - Felixstowe | Whitacre Jct. | |
| 118 | 66603 | 6E55, | Kingsbury | - Humber | Burton-on-Trent | |
| 119 | 60006 | 6T27, | Immingham | - Scunthorpe | Barnetby | |
| 123 | 66170 | 4O20, | Washwood Heath - | Southampton E.D. | Eastleigh | |
| 130 | 56090 | 6M47, | Aldwarke | - Wolverhampton | Whitacre Jct. | |
| 134 | 60001 | 6M46, | Redcar | - Hardendale | Tees Yard | |
| 138 | 57003 | 4O51, | Cardiff Wentloog - | Millbrook | South Moreton | |
| 145 | 37174 | 6D78, | Healey Mills | - Neville Hill | Horbury Cutting | |
| 149 | 66708 | 6Y19, | Mountfield | - Southampton W.D. | Eastleigh | |
| 150 | 60044 | 6D65, | Doncaster | - Immingham | Kirk Sandall | |